SMALL STEPS TO BIG READING

SMALL STEPS TO BIG READING

Converting Non-readers into Readers

Hozefa A Bhinderwala

B L O O M S B U R Y

NEW DELHI • LONDON • OXFORD • NEW YORK • SYDNEY

First published in India 2016
This export edition published in 2020

ISBN 978-93-86141-36-1

Bloomsbury Publishing India Pvt. Ltd
Second Floor, LSC Building No.4
DDA Complex, Pocket C – 6 & 7, Vasant Kunj
New Delhi 110070
www.bloomsbury.com

Typeset by Manipal Digital Systems

PREFACE

Compared to three decades ago, before the advent of the personal computers, the number of people who took to serious reading of books is certainly on the decline. One cannot deny the fact that the value of reading in today's changing times has drastically dropped. This dearth of book reading exists across all ages, but mostly by the parents of school-going children. Some common comments heard every day include:

'But I am not a reader.'

'Just read for my exams. Anything extra, Count me out.'

'Are you crazy? Reading is not for me.'

'If I had been a reader, I'd probably be doing something else.'

'Big fat books are good for decorating studies and libraries, just not my cup of tea.'

'I wish I could read; I could do so much more with my life.'

'I wish my children would read instead of being stuck on digital screens.'

Many factors nullify the interest in reading very early in life. Some of them could be:

- Rigid family members who impose compulsive reading, regardless of the willingness on part of the children.

- Rivalry with a sibling who is exceptionally good with his/her reading skills
- Having a strict unforgiving authoritative teacher
- Lack of interest in the subject
- Fear of not doing well in the subjects and fear of failure in exams
- Inadequate exposure to interesting and understandable reading material
- Frustration over the fact that though the text matter in books increases as one grows, additional reading skills are never imparted [unlike Mathematics, where after being taught numbers and basic operations (+, −, ÷, and ×), detailed instructions are given for further complicated mathematical operations, and the children are not left by themselves to derive the theories of trigonometry]
- Often overlooked and under-diagnosed conditions; a genuine difficulty with reading today acknowledged as dyslexia
- Lack of encouragement and motivation during early reading years

Multitude of factors from the above-mentioned list may be responsible for you not having taken to reading seriously.

In this book, we are therefore, trying to achieve three simple objectives:

1. To encourage non-regular readers to take to reading a little more.
2. To enhance present reading speed of the readers.
3. To enhance the comprehension level of the readers, without which reading serves no purpose.

The fact that you have read this preface means that you are a person who believes in upgrading one's own self and is willing to do that little extra to add quality to life. By coming this far, you have already started your journey in achieving the first objective.

To achieve objectives no. 2 and 3 will be quite a challenge though. I am not a Statistician or a cruncher of numbers, but when you start reading more in less time, your brain relishes the larger understanding of the subject matter and releases endorphins (which are feel-good hormones) that give a very relaxing and soothing feeling to the person. After finishing the first three chapters, if you continue to the fourth, that would imply that you are having fun and there wouldn't be any leftovers between the covers of this book. You will read the entire book.

I assure you that the reading you do after completing this book will be with renewed interest and curiosity. Moreover, you will start reading much more than you previously ever did. In addition, you will benefit more from your reading and overcome many of your previously held limited notions. Once you have achieved this much, it would mean the accomplishment of the other two objectives.

Throughout this book, masculine gender is used to refer to the readers—more out of convenience and to prevent excessive verbiage. Readers may please note that he/she can be interchangeably used, and therefore this should not be seen as any sexist bias.

ACKNOWLEDGEMENTS

Allah, whose guidance, will, and faith, have put it into my system to try, and work on this project.

An enormous thanks for all his providence—be it material, intellectual and spiritual, for it is He who does and provides while we try to take credit for what we achieve.

My Mother, Shirinbai, who fostered the need for education at all costs. She was herself willing to learn the English language even in her late 40s, setting an example. She did not mind sitting behind ten-year-old children with her husband, in the neighbourhood night school.

My Father, Sheikh Abbasbhai, who enkindled optimism in my spirit. His faith in the Almighty and the belief that all problems can be solved with a will to try have been energisers for life. When asked if I could do something big, his response—’If it is good and has not yet been done, it means, you should be the one doing it,’ still ring loudly in my ears every time I have to fight self-doubt.

My Brothers:
Shk Shabbirbhai, Saifeebhai, M Kutbuddinbhai and **Mustafabhai** who sacrificed their education very early on so that the younger

brothers would get the best of it and who supported Dad in consolidating his business. They continue to be my pillars of strength and have always been there for me as role models.

Shk Moizbhai who has been my inspiration for self-belief and his ability to solve problems and do just about anything under the sun.

Shirajbhai, whose multifaceted talents and amazing patience have shaped my earlier childhood. A friend to talk to and the kind of ideal sounding board without whom this life is incomplete.

My Sisters-in-law:
Nafisabhabhi, Munirabhabhi, Rummanabhabhi and **Faridabhabhi,** who prevented my collapse after the early demise of my mother, and did everything in and beyond their reach to ensure I wouldn't be considered a motherless child. They always encouraged me in my academic pursuits.

Rababbhabhi and **Naseemabhabhi**, who though, they were away geographically always supported my educational goals.

My Teacher:
Mr Joel D'Souza, who has been very generous to proofread the manuscript, and has taught me that learning is an ongoing process. His command over the English language and its nuances are second only to God.

My Art Team:
Mrs Kavita Nitin Takane and **Ms Jumana Attari** for their beautiful illustrations, which have breathed life and soul into this collection of words and made it worth picking up.

My Back Office:

My wife **Tasneem,** my kids—**Fatema** and **Taher**, my niece **Zainab Kader** for guiding me put the illustrations and text in place and helping me retain my sanity despite of the chaos all around me, what with the demands of clinical practice and only 24 hours per day.

Lastly, but most importantly, the Staff at Bloomsbury

Mr. Mahendra Lodha, who was open to and accepted the concept.

Mr. Praveen Tiwari, who I have hounded and occasionally harassed with my impulsivity, and was still patient and supportive.

Mr. Arvind Booni, whose brainstorming and positive promotional concepts infused new energy in me.

Mr. Nitin Valecha and **Ms. Ila Garg,** under whose watchful eyes, the book has been scrupulously edited.

The **Other Here Unnamed Staff** at Bloomsbury who have helped my thoughts get inked and printed on paper.

CONTENTS

S. no.		Page No.
	Preface	v
	Acknowledgements	ix
1	Small Steps To Big Goals—A Fresh Start	1
2	What Reading Is and Isn't	12
3	Simplifying The Reading Mechanics	18
4	The Brain and Reading—The Purpose Sought	23
5	Knowing Where To Go—Preview Before Anything Else	28
6	Recording The Experience—Note Taking and Recollecting	34
7	Minimising Self-talk—Read Only, Don't Talk	39
8	Shutting Out Distractions—Launching off to Speed	46

9	Getting Across Quick—Don't Be A Cow, Chew Less	54
10	Speed Kills Distractions—Just Read Fast	64
11	Emboldening Confidence—By Increasing Vocabulary	72
12	Believing In Self—Comprehension Will Catch Up	78
13	Regular Practice—Sharpens Skill, Authoritative Feel	85
14	Different Reading Material	91
15	The Reading Environment	94
16	Enjoying The Benefits—Growing Ahead Fast	99
17	Sharing The Skill—Maintaining The Habit	105
18	Further Reading Enhancement	109
	About The Author	111

1 SMALL STEPS TO BIG GOALS – A FRESH START

So Far So Good, Why Change?

Everybody is aware of the benefits of being a regular reader. In spite of this insight, the average not-so-regular reader believes that if he has managed to come to this point in life without habitual reading, he can get through the remainder of his life without it. This approach is very similar to the people who believe in the existence of God, but are not willing to put in the extra time and effort to either offer prayers or visit a place of worship regularly. 'The Almighty has taken care of me thus; He will look after me later also.' Besides, trying to adapt to any change would mean getting out of the pre-set comfort zone and becoming uncomfortable. Then perhaps struggle a bit in order to regain the original composure. Now who would want to do that?

Being A Reader Is Always Better

Somewhere deep inside, there is a voice that keeps reminding this average not-so-regular reader of how he could do better with even a slight change in his non-reading habits. With growing age and experience, this voice keeps getting louder and clearer until it becomes an unavoidable realisation. When such non-readers finally have the realisation to accomplish something important and are determined to put in the required efforts—that would be the first step towards the goal of being a reader.

Acting On Intent

After garnering awareness and developing a keen intent, the next thing to have ready is a plan of action towards the set goal. You must have observed that very often, you start something, but do not pursue it further—either because there is no plan or because the planning is very huge and unrealistic. In case of reading, it is not how much you read, but how much you relish and benefit from your reading, which should be the milestone for mapping progress in your reading endeavours.

Never Too Late To Start

Whether you are a student in high school, a teacher, a job applicant or an executive officer, you are well aware of the benefits of being a well-read person. At the end of the day, if you have read a bit more than your previous accomplishment, you have begun well. In fact, the more important thing here is to maintain your reading habit. After all, acquiring information and being better informed will always stand you in good stead. This is enough reinforcement to keep you persistent with your newly developed interest in reading.

Villains Of Reading

There are several roadblocks, which will take you away from reading.

The obvious distractions known to all are:

- Technological:
  - Television
  - Computer games
  - Internet
  - Texting on cell-phones

  - Instant messenger
  - Digital Social Media networking
- Non-technological
  - Chilling with friends
  - Social events
  - Lazing around

These are external factors that one can gradually become aware of and then consciously try to avoid them. With a little carefulness, one can actually minimise them.

Fighting the villains. Let us first deal with the obvious conscious distractions.

Honestly, technology is innovative and attention grabbing, and therefore it can easily be a hurdle in the path of your reading. However, one should understand that this exciting technology is still going to hang around even tomorrow and would not ever disappear. For now, your priority should be to fight the seduction of technology that lures you away from what you need to do, what will benefit you in shaping your future.

Acquire the information that you need right now to move ahead in life and do not postpone it for later as even a slightest of delay in this acquisition of information can cost you a better grade, a better job prospect, and at times a life changing opportunity.

We all know how important it is to do the right things at the right time and yet we choose to ignore it. Therefore, I am leaving behind a warning sign in the form of an illustration (*Fig 1.1*) that you can photocopy, and leave on your table, or wherever it is that you sit down to read. This will serve as a physical reminder of your ultimate goal.

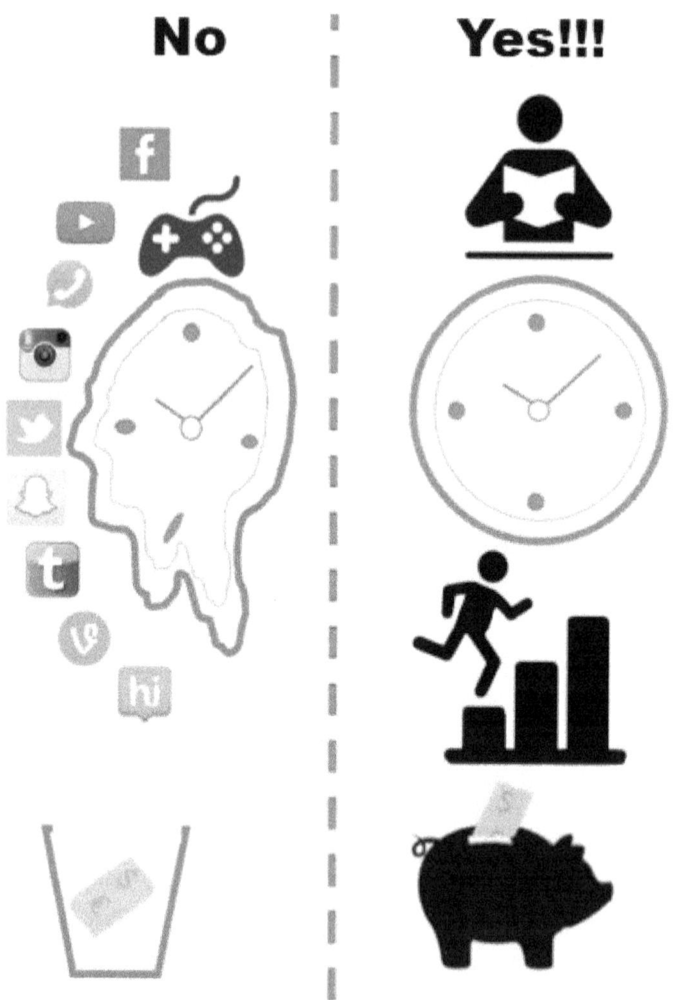

Fig. 1.1 Poster of Time Wasters

Successful people's strategy against distractions. Great people, who have achieved success, often use a similar strategy when it comes to keeping away from distractions and achieving their goals. A very popular hotelier Conrad Hilton attributed his success in career to the power of setting up a goal and then working diligently towards it.

During the Depression of the early 1930s, Hilton's personal financial state was in a mess. He came across a photograph of the Waldorf hotel in a magazine—with its multiple kitchens, hundreds of cooks, waiters and 2000 rooms. He cut out that picture and wrote on it, 'The Greatest of Them All', and placed it in his wallet as a reminder and a constant motivator. When his finances improved and he had a desk again, he slipped the picture under the glass-top of the desk. Thereafter, it was always in front of him.

Fig. 1.2 Image of Goal as a Reminder

Eighteen years later, Conrad Hilton finally acquired the Waldorf. That picture gave Hilton's dream a shape and a substance that kept him focused upon it at all times. Every time he got distracted or distraught, he knew he had no time to let his mind wander for that would take him away from achieving his actual goal.

You could do a similar thing by putting a picture of what you hope to become or what you hope to acquire on your desktop—physical or digital. The illustration (*Fig 1.2*) provided in this book will serve as a reminder to get you back on track, once your mind wanders away from your priority task of reading.

Instinctive Roadblocks To Reading

Here are three of the most disturbing factors, which take us away from our reading habits:

A) **Newton's first law** which states that a body continues to be in its preferred state of rest or motion; here, referred to as the non-reading state.

B) **Guilt** that comes up from not having achieved a personally set target. This tends to grow more and more with every passing minute.

C) **Comparing** what we have achieved with what a friend, classmate, colleague, or co-worker has achieved.

Dealing with these 'disturbing' factors. Now that we have identified the factors that act as hurdles in our reading, we must find a way to overcome them.

Newton's first law. In earlier times, when monarchy prevailed, kings and princes had the luxury of living their lives according to their mood and do things when they wanted to, unlike the present day where what is necessary at the moment has to be attended to immediately, whether we are in the mood for it or not.

Psychological research has provided enough evidence on how we can change our moods by our wilful thinking and deliberate intent. Studies reveal that if you start working on something that you may not be in the mood for; in a matter of time you would actually start developing interest in what you have started. As that unpleasant but important task is initiated, the emotions associated with it gradually change from negative to positive. The importance of the task-at-hand often drives a person to finish off the task in time.

JF10 approach. The 'JF10 approach' is a very simple technique that many 'Time-management Gurus' recommend in order to fight procrastination. This approach says that whatever it is that you have been putting off to do later or not willing to start at all, tell yourself that you will do it for only ten minutes, after which you would stop doing it.

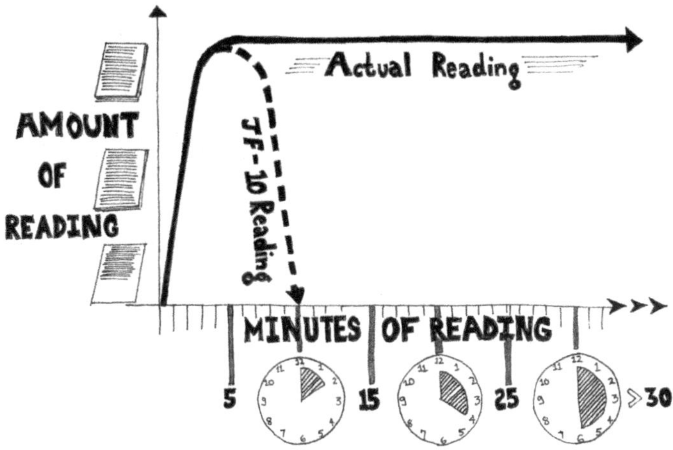

Fig. 1.3 JF 10 – just for 10 Minutes

Our brain works in a funny way—first, it makes excuses for not doing a thing and then decides to continue doing it after ten minutes. You will notice that when you have spent the first five minutes on reading something, and you tell yourself that you will read just for ten minutes (JF10)—you never actually stop. However, you decide to stretch it for a few more minutes. Please note, whenever it is that you decide to stop; be it after ten minutes or more, you will have to put in some time and effort in reading what otherwise you would not have initiated at all.

In a majority of cases, people who have read for the first ten minutes continue reading because of a sense of victory of having defeated their own negativity (*Fig 1.3*). Thus, you will be able to surpass the first hurdle and go on to conquer other barriers.

Guilt. Now, the guilt that comes up from not having achieved a personally set target is an innate human emotion. It saps our major chunk of time and energy. Those who do not feel any guilt are either psychologically ill or have an anti-social personality. So if you experience guilt frequently, welcome to the club of 'normal people'.

But why is guilt so necessary? Well, it prevents you from doing certain things which are ethically, morally or socially unacceptable. Without guilt, our world would be full of chaos and anarchy. Even in the smallest of doses, it is thus, a great motivator to stop doing the wrong things and take corrective measures in order to rectify the wrong doing (if any).

So problem only arises when this guilt persists for long; it is then that it starts freezing our senses and pushes us from action to inaction. How can we bury this lasting guilt? There is a four-step-process to overcome guilt (*Fig 1.4*) that can eventually help us to not only be guilt-ridden but also move further with our set goal.

Step 1: Identification

It is imperative to first start acknowledging its presence. Once identified, we need to bid farewell to it before it starts growing big inside us. We should accept guilt with conviction, and say this to ourselves, 'Yes, I am guilty for what I have done. And I do not wish to continue feeling guilty about it. Instead, I need to take corrective steps. I do not have the time or energy to continue brooding over it and feeling bad for myself. I have only enough energy to move ahead. Bye-bye guilt.'

Step 2: Flush it out

Whatever you are doing at that time, take a break and drink a glass of water. It would function as if you are washing off the guilt out of your system, and in that process discarding it completely. Yes, there is actually a scientific explanation for this action. What happens is, when we experience guilt, we also experience intense anxiety along with it. It causes dryness of mouth and throat. In this situation, drinking water physiologically tackles symptoms of anxiety and cures it.

It is therefore advisable to get up and move away from wherever you are at the time of guilt. Take a brisk walk for at least two minutes.

This would work as if you are leaving your guilt far behind. Next, make a trip to the restroom and relieve your bladder. This way, you end up relieving yourself of any further stress physiologically, and then the mind resumes its role as if it has been reset. You don't have to take my word for this technique—use it and see for yourself how easy it is to defeat guilt.

Fig. 1.4 Overcoming Guilt of Not Reading

Step 3: Just get back

Once you are done with cleansing your system out of guilt, resume your reading activity. Remind yourself of how fortunate you are to get back on track, and minimise the amount of time and energy that you would have otherwise wasted on brooding over guilt.

Step 4: A pat on the back

After five minutes of having re-initiated reading, give yourself a big pat on the back for successfully leaving the guilt behind and getting on with your task-at-hand. You have now won a psychological duel all by yourself and are a victor in true sense.

Comparing. Many-a-times, we tend to compare our achievements with that of a friend, classmate, colleague, or competitor. This often mars the excitements of our own achievements. So when you find yourself comparing your progress with anyone else's, you need to ask yourself these three questions:

1. Are you benefitting in any way by this comparison?
2. Is this comparison getting more of your work accomplished or helping you get it finished in a better way?
3. Is the person you are comparing yourself with in your exact same place or is his situation different from yours?

Do you think that all these three questions would be answered with merely a 'no'? Your compulsion to compare has to be responded to by these affirmations. You should say them to yourself as many times as you can:

'I will only benefit by my own effort, and I will strive to work diligently from here on.'

'What anyone else does is good for them, what I do is good for me. I am happy for all of us.'

'I am unique in my own way and there is only one me in this universe. Also, unique are my circumstances and position. Let me not try and be anyone else. An original is better than a cheap imitation. Let me be the best 'me' that I can be. I will not let my value be reduced by being compared to anyone else. At least, not in my mind.'

Most often inertia, guilt, and comparisons stop us from our reading and many other tasks in life simply because of our perceived helplessness. The moment we can identify these factors and question their presence, we start overcoming them and are on our way of doing much more with our lives.

2 WHAT READING IS AND ISN'T – CRUSHING FALSE NOTIONS

No.	Belief	Clarification
1	Your natural reading speed is unmodifiable (*Fig 2.1*)	There is no such thing as a natural reading speed. Like any other skill, it can be learned, honed and improved upon with regular practice.

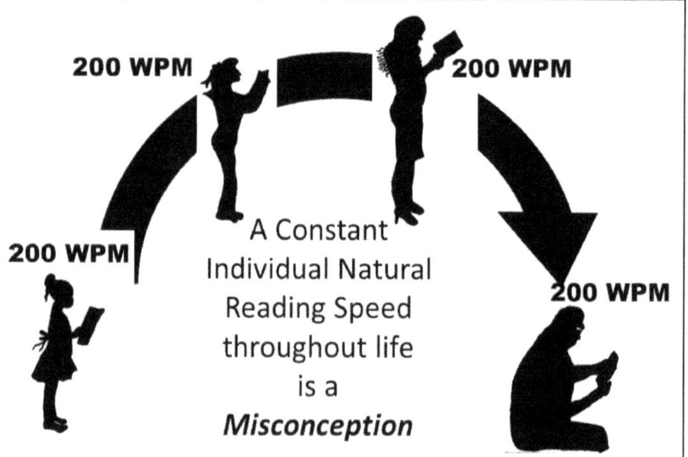

Fig. 2.1 The Myth of Unmodifiable Natural Reading Speed

2	Reading at a fast pace reduces your understanding and eventually you waste more time in re-reading	When you read fast, chances of getting distracted are minimised—allowing better focus and therefore better comprehension (*Fig 2.2*). This actually helps you read more in less time, thereby saving time instead of wasting it.

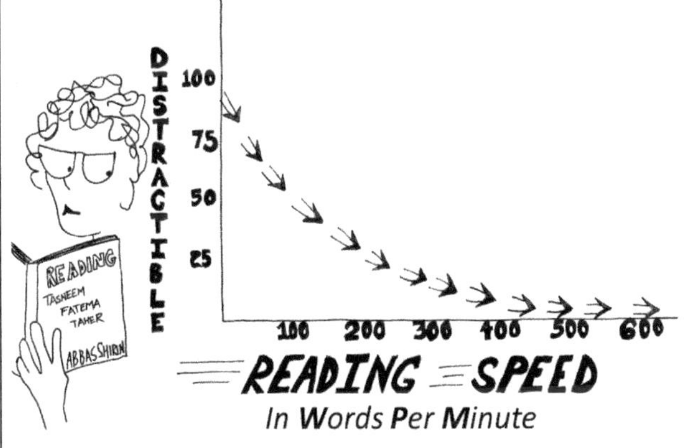

Fig. 2.2 Reading Fast Reduces Distractibility

3	For better understanding you should read slowly	The slower you read, higher the chances of your eyes losing their place in the line because of irregular eye movements. Also, it predisposes your brain to more distraction.

<table>
<tr><td>4</td><td>Only if your eyes can focus on every printed word, you will understand what you're reading</td><td>Even if the eyes miss a few words, (Fig 2.3) the brain can make sense of what is being conveyed by the gist of the remainder of the paragraph.</td></tr>
<tr><td colspan="3"> 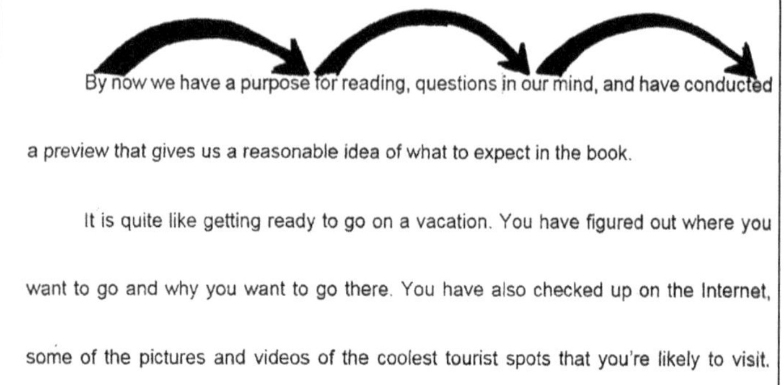By now we have a purpose for reading, questions in our mind, and have conducted a preview that gives us a reasonable idea of what to expect in the book.

It is quite like getting ready to go on a vacation. You have figured out where you want to go and why you want to go there. You have also checked up on the Internet, some of the pictures and videos of the coolest tourist spots that you're likely to visit.
Fig. 2.3 Even if the eyes skip a few words</td></tr>
<tr><td>5</td><td>You would not understand and remember if you do not hear what you have been reading</td><td>In primary school, you were still familiarising yourself with new words. Beyond primary school years, you do not need to hear what you read to understand as your vocabulary has expanded considerably. Reading is clearly not a hearing dependent function.</td></tr>
</table>

6	The faster you move your tongue while you read, the better your reading speed becomes	The tongue is a highly muscular organ which is unnecessary for reading. It's movement limits your ability of reading to less than 300 words per minute. Also, reading requires only the eyes, the optic nerve and the brain to be actively involved. By moving the tongue, we reduce brain's resources available for reading as now the brain has to focus on moving the tongue.
7	You should attempt to remember hundred per cent of what you read	It is virtually impossible to try and remember hundred per cent of what you read. It is not only extremely difficult, but unnecessary. As long as the gist of what is read is understood and remembered, it's sufficient.
8	Your eyes should flow in a continuous sweeping moment across the line as you read	Our eyes move across the line of print in jerky movements, called saccades, not in flowing rhythmic movements. This is due to the small strap muscles which move by tugging at the eyeballs which give it a jerky motion.

9	If you miss something while reading, you should go back to make sure you have read and understood what you missed, before you go on further (*Fig 2.4*)	It is the meaning that is being conveyed in the paragraph that is more important than the individual words that are printed. Every word is not important. Every time you go back to re-read, it becomes exhausting for the brain as the comprehension also suffers in the process.

Going back for missed words

a preview that gives us a reasonable idea of what to expect in the book.

It is quite like getting ready to go on a vacation. You have figured out where you want to go and why you want to go there. You have also checked up on the Internet, some of the pictures and videos of the coolest tourist spots that you're likely to visit.

Fig. 2.4 Going back for Missed Words

10	Only reading about the subject matter is reading; all other reading material is a waste of time.	Reading has to be initiated and then gradually increased. One has to relish the feel of the printed page between the fingers. In case of children, the colourful picture books help them get initiated. Later encyclopaedias, and then books of their interest occupy their bookshelves. So long as they start developing interest in reading, do not question the content. Some reading is definitely better than no reading at all. *Once you acquire a driving license, the type of car you have to drive is not of much consequence.*

3 SIMPLIFYING THE READING PROCESS – UNDERSTANDING THE MECHANICS

Reading requires just two organ systems—those of the eye and brain. The eye to read and the brain to understand what is read.

What Most People Do

Many innocent and ignorant readers end up using other organ systems that have nothing to do with reading (*Fig 3.1*). Most people speak every word they read as they believe that it aids concentration. This way they involve:

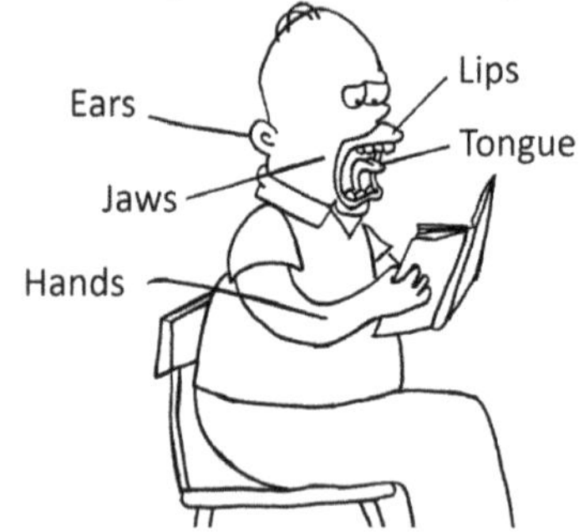

Fig 3.1 Not organs of reading

- the eyes
- the jaws
- the tongue
- the lips
- the ears
- the parts of the brain which are concerned with speaking, hearing and understanding what is heard.

In involving so many organs to read, the reading speed gets seriously affected. It is difficult for the muscular jaws and tongue to keep up the pace of movement for too long and therefore, reading speed is drastically slowed down. Now, at slow reading speeds, the brain tends to get distracted easily, thus, damping the comprehension and the overall pleasure of reading.

Only The Eyes And The Brain

I repeat, the only organs required for reading are the eyes and the part of the brain required to process visual material and interpret language.

When you are travelling in a vehicle along the highway, you read the advertisements on hoardings and various directions without having to say them aloud or placing your hands on those words. You only need to read them with your eyes and understand them with your brain.

Let us take a look at the pictures of the areas of the brain involved when a person speaks and the areas of the brain involved when a person merely reads (*Fig 3.2* and *Fig 3.3*).

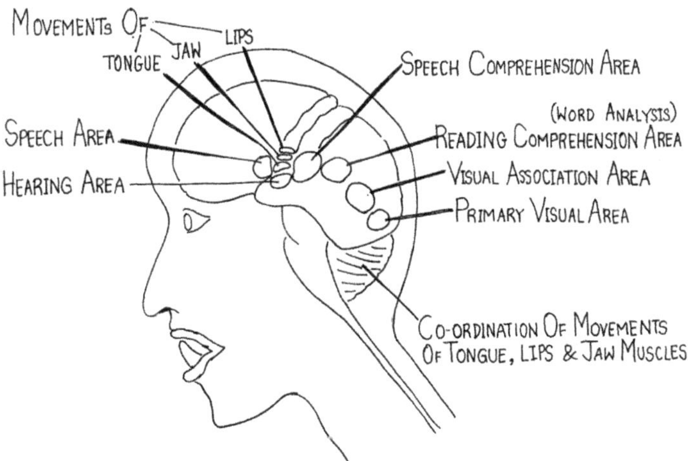

Fig 3.2 Brain areas involved when speaking while reading

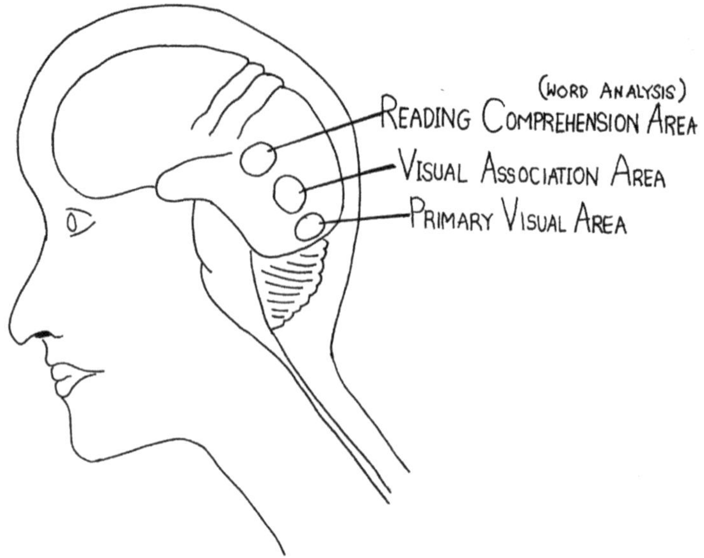

Fig 3.3 Brain areas invovled when only eyes used while reading

Some people use their fingers to point at and move along every word that they are reading. Now, here also brain's resources are being used to move and co-ordinate a variety of larger muscle groups instead of simply moving the eyes and the part of the brain that is responsible for processing information.

The Full Process Of Reading: Fixations And Saccades

Let us understand the process of reading in a little more detail.

The reader sees a printed word on a line. The eye snaps up the picture of that word and sends an image of the printed word, very quickly (pacing between 100-400 km/hour) to that portion of the brain where what is seen is understood.

This information is then processed between the visual area of the brain and the language processing area of the brain. The instant (within milliseconds) this is understood, the brain signals the eyes to move across the right side of the line of print (to the left if the reader is reading Urdu/Arabic) to capture an image of the second word. The whole process is repeated until you reach the end of the line. The capturing of the word at any point by the eyes is referred to as a 'fixation' and the movement (the jump) of the eye from one word to the next is referred to as a 'saccade' (*Fig 3.4*).

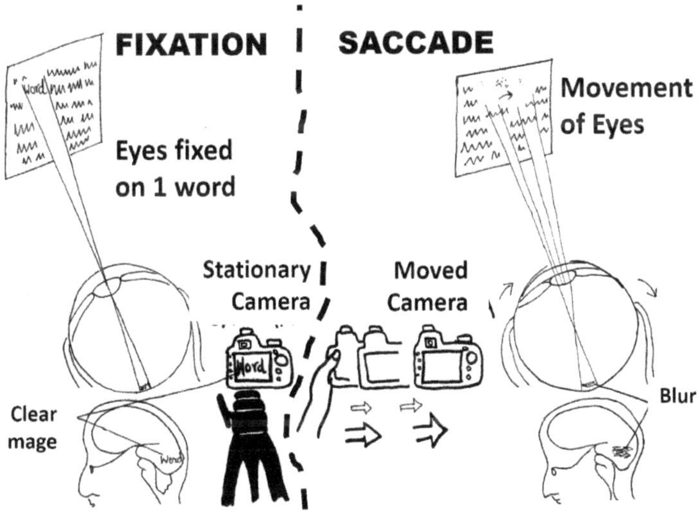

Fig 3.4 A Fixation & a Saccade

The Eye Like A Camera

This is quite similar to using a still camera. When the camera is held still, a clear image is taken. Similarly, when the eye stops at a fixation, reading occurs. Just like when the still camera moves, a blurred image is formed—when the eye moves during a saccade, no reading occurs.

The eye has an ability to move across the line of print to a maximum of four times per second. Going faster than that is beyond the ability of the tiny strap muscles of the eye. At this rate, while taking one word per fixation, with four fixations per second, our reading speed will be limited to less than 240 words per minute.

The Eye Movements in Speed-reading

Speed-reading is not about moving the eye at a fast pace per second. It is about capturing more words per fixation. So we need to master the art of moving across the line of print quickly with confidence, knowing that though we haven't made fixations at every word of print on the line, our eyes have sent all the words on the line to the brain.

It sounds very far-fetched initially to the reader that he/she may be able to take in more than one word per fixation. In reality, however, the readers have already done so hundreds of times in their lives when they read just before exams.

4 THE BRAIN AND READING – THE PURPOSE SOUGHT

What Did You Just Read?

Many a times, it happens that after we have read a page, an article or a chapter in a book and we are absolutely clueless about what we have read in the end. Doesn't it sound familiar?

The reading that we did in primary school normally involved reading a chapter and then answering questions at the end of the chapter (*Fig 4.1*). It was expected that we understand the content of the chapter and are able to answer any questions thereafter.

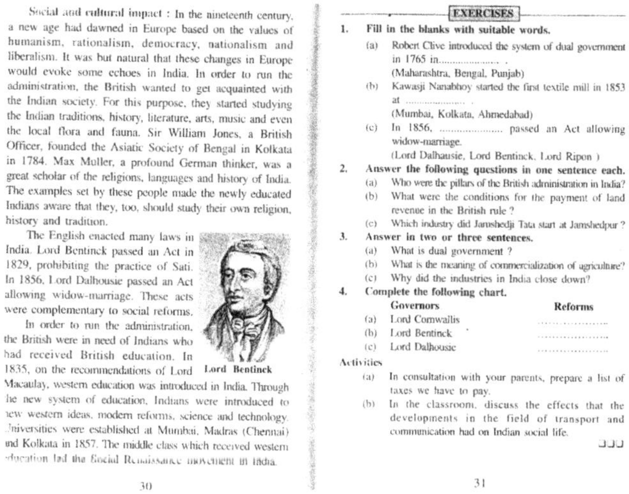

Social and cultural impact : In the nineteenth century, a new age had dawned in Europe based on the values of humanism, rationalism, democracy, nationalism and liberalism. It was but natural that these changes in Europe would evoke some echoes in India. In order to run the administration, the British wanted to get acquainted with the Indian society. For this purpose, they started studying the Indian traditions, history, literature, arts, music and even the local flora and fauna. Sir William Jones, a British Officer, founded the Asiatic Society of Bengal in Kolkata in 1784. Max Muller, a profound German thinker, was a great scholar of the religions, languages and history of India. The examples set by these people made the newly educated Indians aware that they, too, should study their own religion, history and tradition.

The English enacted many laws in India. Lord Bentinck passed an Act in 1829, prohibiting the practice of Sati. In 1856, Lord Dalhousie passed an Act allowing widow-marriage. These acts were complementary to social reforms.

Lord Bentinck

In order to run the administration, the British were in need of Indians who had received British education. In 1835, on the recommendations of Lord Macaulay, western education was introduced in India. Through the new system of education, Indians were introduced to new western ideas, modern reforms, science and technology. Universities were established at Mumbai, Madras (Chennai) and Kolkata in 1857. The middle class which received western education led the Social Renaissance movement in India.

30

EXERCISES

1. **Fill in the blanks with suitable words.**
   (a) Robert Clive introduced the system of dual government in 1765 in...................... .
   (Maharashtra, Bengal, Punjab)
   (b) Kawasji Nanabhoy started the first textile mill in 1853 at ....
   (Mumbai, Kolkata, Ahmedabad)
   (c) In 1856, ... passed an Act allowing widow-marriage.
   (Lord Dalhausie, Lord Bentinck, Lord Ripon)
2. **Answer the following questions in one sentence each.**
   (a) Who were the pillars of the British administration in India?
   (b) What were the conditions for the payment of land revenue in the British rule ?
   (c) Which industry did Jamshedji Tata start at Jamshedpur ?
3. **Answer in two or three sentences.**
   (a) What is dual government ?
   (b) What is the meaning of commercialization of agriculture?
   (c) Why did the industries in India close down?
4. **Complete the following chart.**

	Governors	Reforms
(a)	Lord Cornwallis	....
(b)	Lord Bentinck	....
(c)	Lord Dalhousie	....

Activities

(a) In consultation with your parents, prepare a list of taxes we have to pay.
(b) In the classroom, discuss the effects that the developments in the field of transport and communication had on Indian social life.

❑❑❑

31

Fig 4.1 Exercise at the end of Chapter in School Text Books

Of Interest Or Not

If the chapter had a story or a subject that appealed to us or grabbed our interest, that implies we were reading keenly while forming connections and associations in our brain about stuff we already knew. However, if for any reason the material we were reading didn't excite us, that means we just went through it without giving focused attention on what we were gazing at with our eyes (*Fig 4.2*).

Fig 4.2 Disinterested Reader

This way, we end up reading a lot of material without understanding and forming new associations in the brain. Our eyes feel that they had moved down the page, but the brain is often lost somewhere else, distracted and thinking of something else. The stuff we read, thus looks meaningless.

When Asked What You Read

When the time to respond to questions comes, the disinterested and lost reader stares blankly. The interrogator (be it the parent, the teacher or the examiner) does not understand why the reader did not grasp the topic, gets upset and cannot show acknowledgement of the lack of interest. On the contrary, they display a gesture of disapproval which is generally expressed by unkind words, and often, punishments (*Fig 4.3*).

Fig 4.3 When asked what you just read

The Unhappy Reader

Fig 4.4 Student developing aversion to reading

This baffles the lost reader and instead of motivating him to do well, it pushes him into a feeling where he believes that he would be happier without that particular person as well as that subject. If this continues, the reader becomes more averse to the subject and gradually to the activity that associates with the subject—here, reading (*Fig 4.4*).

This is one of the reasons, many students don't like to read a particular subject or are absolutely disinterested in what they read.

Purpose: The Saviour

To counter this, and to keep the lack of interest in reading at bay, it helps 'to have a purpose' of reading a book or any other text that we have in front of us. What we need to do is to ask ourselves a few questions about what we are about to read.

'Why am I reading this?'

'Do I need to read this now?'

'What is it that I seek to understand from this reading?'

Your other questions should be subject-specific. For this, you should be aware about the topic-at-hand, e.g., if you're reading about an event in history, it helps to formulate a few questions like:

'What time period did this event occur in?'

'Who were the key people responsible for the event?'

'Why did this event occur in the first place?'

'How did this event change the existing circumstances?'

'Could this event have turned out differently?'

'What are the implications of this event, if any, in the present-day scenario?'

Write Down Your Questions

Once you have written down these questions on a piece of paper, you have already prepared your brain to start seeking answers. Thereafter, whatever you do with your reading will have a purpose. When you will sit down to read, your brain will now look for answers, and would not get lost, or bored in the process. This is because there is an unfinished business at hand which keeps the brain motivated (*Fig 4.5*).

If you find it difficult to formulate your own questions or purpose, it helps to first read the exercise or set of questions placed at the end of the chapter as that will make you feel like a detective, who is seeking clues on an unknown mission. Try it for yourself, and you will see how it works wonders.

Fig 4.5 Interested Reader

5 KNOWING WHERE TO GO – PREVIEW BEFORE ANYTHING ELSE

Comfortable With What You Know

You must have noticed that mostly we prefer going to places we know about and doing things we have at least a slight idea of. An occasional element of surprise while visiting a new place on a vacation is a welcome thought, but to have to go to unfamiliar places every now and then usually becomes a stressful activity. Even if we do not know details of the place, just having been there once is good enough as it gives us some degree of confidence. We have an image of what to expect ready in our mind, which helps us relish the place when we visit it next.

Fig 5.1 Clear directions of route

First-time Visitor

If we are going to a place for the first time, a knowledge about the directions with specific landmarks comes as handy and help us to locate and reach the destination without any hassle (*Fig 5.1*). the unavailability of proper landmarks or signposts (*Fig 5.2*) could prove to be a trouble. It's a tiresome task having to ask for directions time and again, not to mention the unavoidable delay.

Fig 5.2 Landmarks

The experience of travelling to a new place is very similar to reading. Whenever a reader starts reading something new; a new topic, chapter or book, it has a somewhat exciting and sometimes daunting, occasionally intimidating feeling, because of the unfamiliarity of the new content. This is usually much less threatening when the book or subject has recently been accessed or is of immense interest to the reader.

Front Cover **Back Cover**

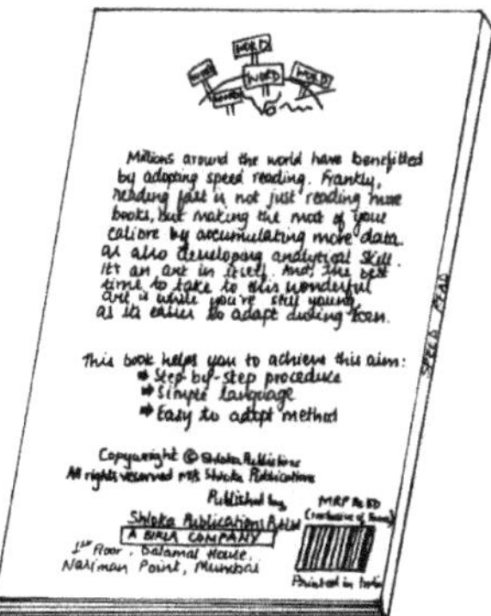

Fig 5.3 Front cover and the back cover of the book

Welcome To Previewing

The good news is that there is a way of minimising this threatening-feeling voluntarily, and that is by visiting the content or the book even before you actually set out to start reading it. This is referred to as 'previewing'.

What you do in previewing is that you take an overview of the book at a much brisker rate than you would if you were actually reading it. Here is how you do it:

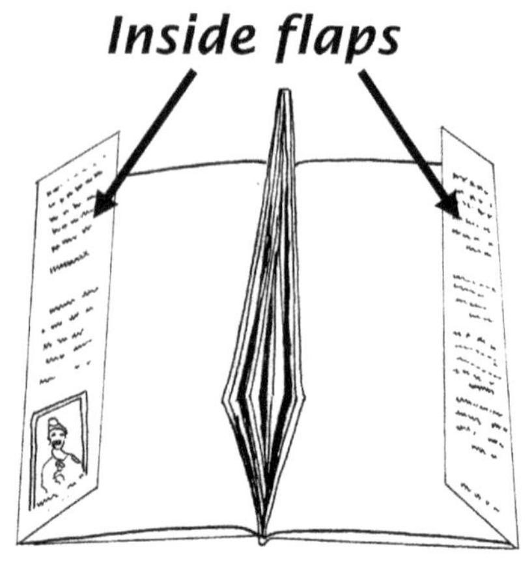

Fig 5.4 Inside flaps of the book

- At first, you look at the cover, the back cover (*Fig 5.3*), and the flaps (*Fig 5.4*), if there are any. This tells you precisely, what you might find in the book. It also gives you an idea of the author, the content, and the kind of people that may have felt it necessary to say something about the book, and what they may have said about it.
- Then you open the book, and quickly glance through to read the table of contents (*Fig 5.5*).

Table of Contents

Fig 5.5 Table of Contents of the book

This gives you the framework of the book, and a reasonable understanding of how the entire content has been split up into smaller components. Sometimes, it may be possible to localise a particular chapter of keen interest that may hold the answer to questions you have in your mind. If the book is not written in a continuous flowing manner, then you can decide to go to the specific chapter and get the required information. This will save a good amount of your time by eliminating some of the other chapters that may be unimportant or irrelevant to you.

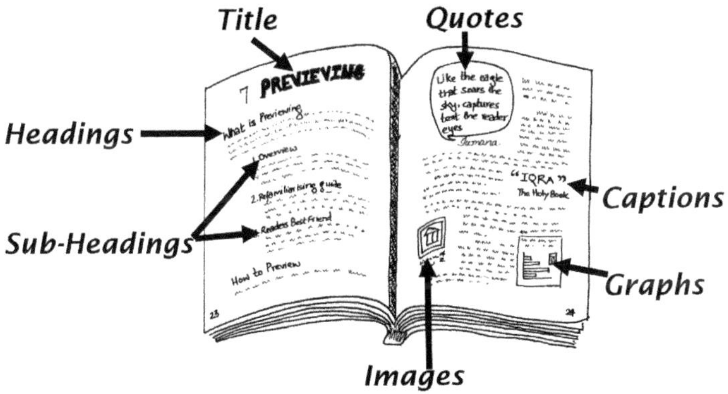

Fig 5.6 Headings, Emphatic points and illustrations

- Now you jump into the flesh of the book and start turning the pages, as if you were just looking for headings, titles, and other highlighted matter on the pages (*Fig 5.6*), illustrations, graphs, tables, photographs, quotations or pictures (*Fig 5.7*).

Fig 5.7 Tables, Flow Charts, Cartoons

You can allow yourself about five to twenty seconds per page, and thumb through the whole book varying your pace, depending on what the contents of the pages are (*Fig 5.8*). This gives you a look around of the matter and a reasonable feel of the entire material. The illustrations, cartoons and pictures, tell the readers that the author is concerned about expressing himself more visually and is keen to hold the reader's attention. A non-reader or an amateur-reader is more likely to pick up such a book to read, as he knows that there will be less text to read per page. The graphs and tables, though occupying just a little space on the page—sometimes, only as a representation, convey the gist of the whole text matter.

- Lastly, you take a quick look at the index, if there is one, to make sure that nothing is missed out.

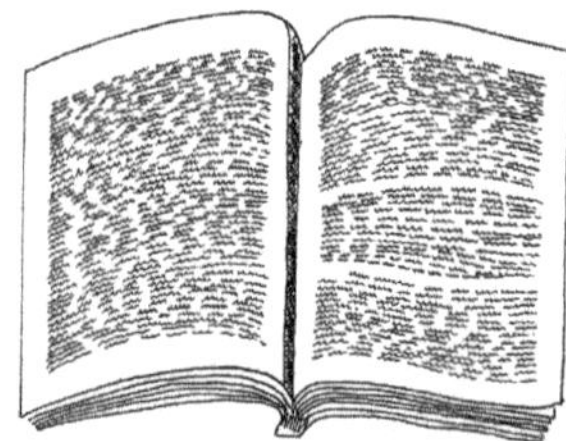

Fig 5.8 Type setting and layout of Print

This has to be done very quickly to see the detail in it to facilitate looking up matter, when needed. It also helps to see if the questions you have in your mind about a particular topic have been indexed or not. This leaves you with a feeling relieved that the matter you have in your hand will be helpful and easy to go through.

Have Been There

When you start the actual reading of matter that you have previewed, there is a sense of familiarity with the content which makes you feel assured and confident about your reading. It is as if your brain is re-visiting a familiar place and you are no lost stranger anymore.

Additionally, a preview opens a window into the matter—allowing the reader to discover something of importance or interest which may help avert a delay in starting to read the subject because of any previous resistance.

Reading Efficiency Enhancer

A preview can also help guide the reader to identify avoidable or unimportant sections of the chapter or book even before beginning. There may be lots of information that may not directly apply to what you are looking for. When you become aware of that during the preview process, you save a lot of precious time and effort that would have otherwise been wasted. Reading from cover to cover is not only exhausting but a useless activity at times. This leads to frustration in the end when the realisation daws upon.

6 RECORDING THE EXPERIENCE – NOTE TAKING AND RECOLLECTING

So far, we have a purpose for reading, questions in our mind, and have conducted a preview that gives us a reasonable idea of what to expect in the book.

Fig 6.1 Previewing a travel destination

Before A Vacation

It is quite similar to getting ready to go on a vacation. You have figured out where you want to go and why you want to go there.

In addition, you have browsed the internet for the pictures and videos of the coolest tourist spots that you're likely to visit during the vacation (*Fig 6.1*). You're likely to do this a few days or maybe a week or two before taking your vacation. If you were to make a note on paper, and make a small plan of how you intend to travel and stay on your vacation, it becomes a lot easier. Right?

Fig 6.2 Plight of not recording preview notes

Wish You Had Saved The Information

Imagine going to a new place, without any clear information or any instructions or maybe having some information but none of it in recorded form (*Fig 6.2*). Between the times you access the information and make your trip, without a written record you can lose out on a lot of precious and relevant information. You may spend more time, effort and money in some random place and lose out on another more exciting place altogether. But when you are investing a large amount of your finances and time, don't you want to do it wisely?

Reinforcing The Preview

Similarly, just keeping the 'preview' in mind is also not enough. Pouring the preview generated in the mind on to the paper is therefore, a very good way of keeping it alive and healthy. Just like the money and time invested on a vacation, the effort and time invested in your reading has to yield good results. For this reason, it makes good sense to make a written note of your understanding of the preview before you proceed any further.

Different Strokes For Different Folks

Everybody has their own unique way of understanding concepts and noting them down. Some people prefer to write down the points, one below the other, while others prefer to make flowcharts or drawings. Many others are likely to make mind maps (*Fig 6.3*). 'Sketch noting' is an interesting way of taking notes, and is worth checking out on the internet. Follow whichever system you wish to, but ensure that at the end of your preview, you spend a few minutes to note down whatever information you have acquired during the process.

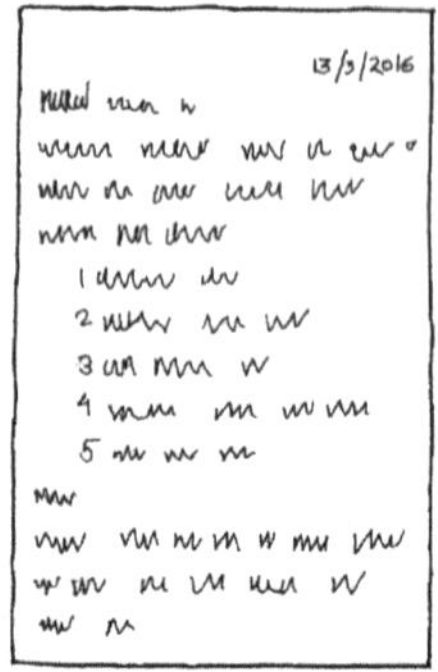
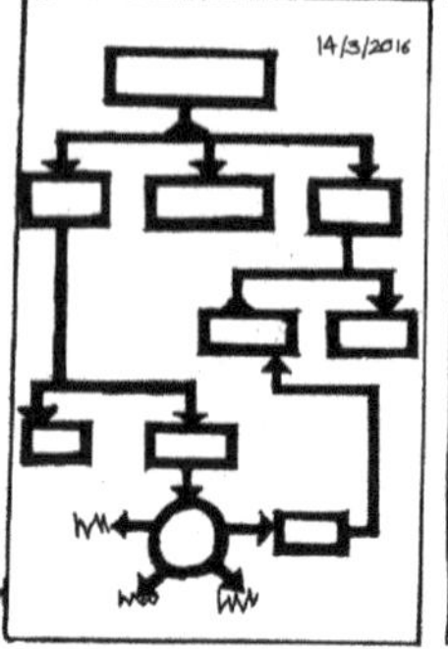
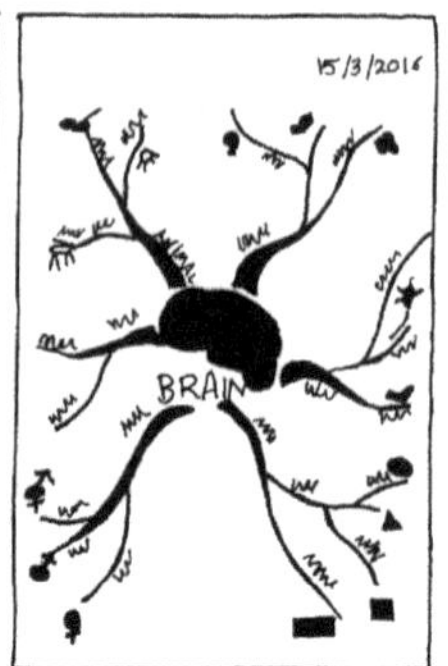

Linear Notes **Flow Charts** **Mind Maps**

Fig 6.3 Types of Notes

Neuropsychological Benefits Of Note Taking

This process of noting down your ideas consolidates the information in your brain. In addition, your eyes are exposed to new information. Every time your brain acquires a new nugget of information, a nerve ending in your brain makes a new association or connection (technically referred to as a 'synapse'). When we go a step further and make a note of what we have previewed, we revisit the new connection, making it stronger and more easily accessible whenever this new information has to be reviewed.

When you are making the notes, try to recollect as much information as possible and record it on paper. If a particular drawing, illustration or graph comes to mind, make a note of it as well. This kind of note taking has the magical ability of making the most boring and dull topics come to life.

Once this is done, in your brain's eye you have already visited the streets of the book, seen the landmarks, acquainted yourself with some of the characters, and know the places of interest in the book. You also have some drawings and pictures of the contents of the book etched in mind.

Relaxed Brain – Better Reading

At this stage, your brain does not have a sense of insecurity or unfamiliarity with the contents of the book. Now, when you pick up the book to read—because of a sense of familiarity, it becomes much easier for your eyes to wade through the book. You will notice that your overall understanding of the text is much enhanced even before you have started reading (*Fig 6.4*).

Your level of stress is definitely lower than what it would have been, had the matter to be read been unfamiliar to you. It is also a plus point in terms of the time saved as now you can quickly get to the most relevant point.

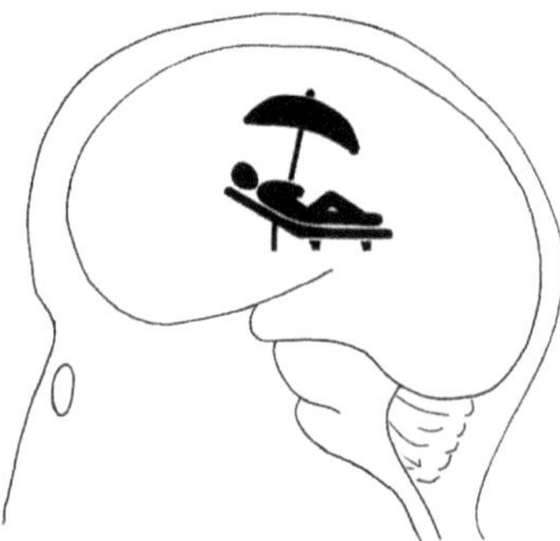

Fig 6.4 Relaxed Brain - Better Reading

A Worthwhile Investment

What you do not know is the amount of time you will save when you do not have to re-read the text. This is because, now you will have a relatively better comprehension of it when you actually set out to read. For many students, a quick glance of just their preview notes, when time is extremely short, is a good enough way to revise their academic material.

7 MINIMISING SELF-TALK – READ ONLY, DON'T TALK

Primary School Teacher's Instructions

When we learned to read in primary school, our teachers insisted that we read every word aloud so that we could hear what we read (*Fig 7.1*). This was very important because at that age, we needed to clear our diction as well as know for sure, how the letters when joined together sound and how they should be pronounced. Also at that time, we had a very limited vocabulary and were in the process of adding to the number of words we knew. Unfortunately, many adults continue reading aloud to hear the words that they are reading (*Fig 7.2*). This often disrupts the flow of reading and mars the effect of the content too.

Fig 7.1 Teacher's instructions to read every word aloud

Fig 7.2 Adults reading every word aloud

Increasing Vocabulary With Age And Experience

Our vocabulary increases with every passing day of acquiring new information and encountering any new text or experience. I am assuming that those of you who are reading this book have at least been readers for more than five years now. Your vocabulary from the time you started reading has multiplied manifold. The unfamiliar words that you come across are very few and infrequent. You can conveniently accelerate your reading speed without the fear of coming across words that you may not know or understand.

Speech On Stage, Not in Reading

The habit of reading aloud every word often has serious consequences on your ability to comprehend the material. When we read aloud, we use the muscles of our tongue, cheeks, jaws, and lips to speak, in addition to the movement of the small muscles of the eyes. The brain now has to focus on moving so many groups of muscles as well as listen to what is being spoken. In an effort to coordinate our speech while reading, our ability to read fast slows down.

Speech While Reading Limits Comprehension

This means, if we're speaking while reading, we're limiting the reading speed to less than 300 words per minute (as mentioned earlier). After the words are sent by the eyes to the brain, it is now the job of the brain to process and make sense of the words that it receives. Reading without understanding is after all a waste of time and effort.

Processing Ability Of The Brain

The Human brain is capable of processing 500+ words per minute. This means that regardless of how many words are sent to the brain, the brain will still process or make sense of at least 500 words per minute. When we read aloud, we limit the sending of the words to the brain by the eyes. Every minute, we send about 200 words less to the brain. This hampers our reading activity to a great extent.

Read Slow And Enhance Distraction And Daydreaming

The brain will fill in this deficit of 200 words that you do not send through your eyes from the printed page, either by some other thoughts of fancy or through distraction from the environment or daydreaming. The brain will process its full quantum of information worth at least 500 words per minute. So when you are reading at a speed of 300 words or less per minute, the brain is thinking of something or other (with the other available 200 words) that may have nothing to do with your reading material. This will lead to unnecessary distraction and mar the comprehension.

Vicious Cycle Of Slow Reading, Distraction And Frustration

Often, the other thoughts overpower the little information that your eyes are sending off to the brain. So, you stop after three paragraphs to wonder what you read in the first two. You then decide to read more slowly and carefully, not realising that you're making it even more difficult for your brain to understand what you are reading. When we read slowly, we have to strain ourselves and put in that extra effort to keep away from distractions, and solely focus on the printed words of the page. This extra effort can hardly be sustained comfortably for more than a few seconds.

After that little time, again the brain goes back to other thoughts—like in a gravitational field any object would fall to the ground, if not held away from the ground. In this manner, by reading slowly, we make it more difficult for the brain to understand. It does not surprise me that so many students and adults alike, get fed up of reading after trying their best to read slowly and carefully.

Give Up Bad Habits To Benefit

The main culprit here is our habit of saying aloud every word we read. This habit, though wonderful for a new reader, should be changed as the reader goes on to acquire a better vocabulary. When you minimise sub-vocalising, you successfully add another 50 to 75 words per minute to your present reading speed.

Fig 7.3 Stick tongue to roof of mouth

Changing a habit can be a little uncomfortable initially, but the benefits of doing so should encourage the reader to be persistent in his efforts. Most people are not even aware that they are sub-vocalising. So we can try and minimise this sub-vocalising, but to give it up totally, is rather challenging.

Overcoming Sub-vocalising

So the first step to overcome sub-vocalising is to catch yourself doing it. Once you become aware, you can think of ways to minimise it.

Here are a few ways that can help you be cognisant of this habit of sub-vocalising:

- Press your tongue upwards towards the roof of your mouth while reading (*Fig 7.3*).

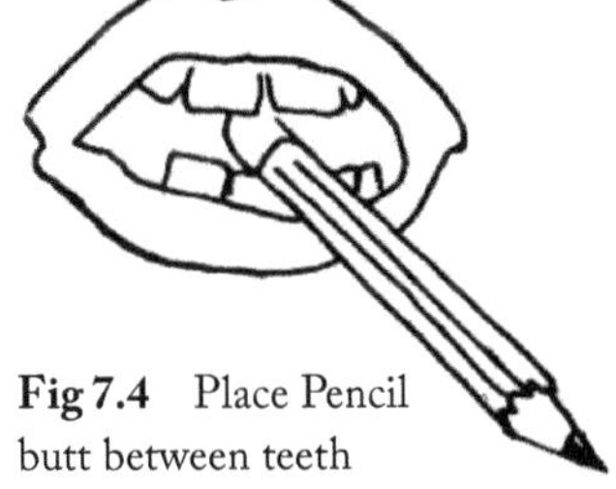

Fig 7.4 Place Pencil butt between teeth

- As you read, place a pencil butt between your teeth as if you were holding a cigarette in your mouth (*Fig 7.4*). (I am, by no means recommending smoking a cigarette as an alternate to overcome sub-vocalising.)
- When you read, bite your tongue gently preventing it from moving around inside your mouth (*Fig 7.5*). You will instantly become aware of the movement of your tongue away from its position when you start to sub-vocalise.

Fig 7.5 Bite tongue gently

- During your reading, press your index finger to your lips as if you were hushing a child to remain quiet (*Fig 7.6*). You will be able to feel the movement of your lips on your fingers when you sub-vocalise and thereby, stop yourself at the right moment.
- Apply a little toothpaste between your lips as if you were sealing your lips with it as you start reading (*Fig 7.7*). As soon as your lips move, your tongue will immediately pop out and taste of the toothpaste will remind you of your sub-vocalising tendency.

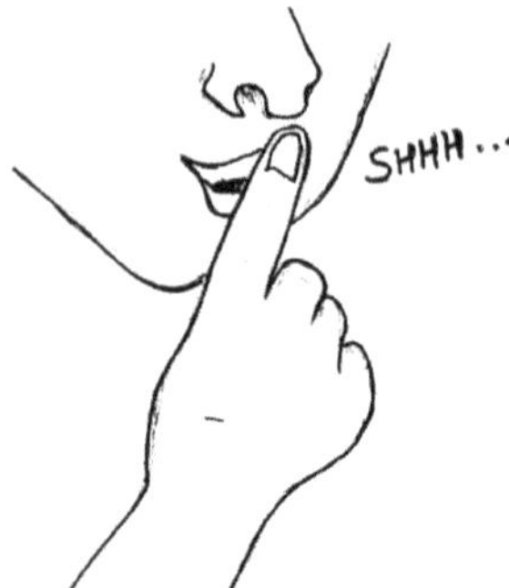

Fig 7.6 Pressing Index finger to lips

Fig 7.7 Apply little Toothpaste on lips

If you're comfortable doing any of these, they can be used to eventually overcome the habit. Gradually you can outgrow it completely.

The Sub-vocalising Killer: Simply Read Fast

The best way to overcome sub-vocalising though, is to simply read so fast that your lips and tongue can no more keep pace with your reading speed. Yes, when you read at a very fast pace, the muscular system of the mouth gives up on keeping up with your reading. Thus, the entire responsibility of reading is left to be done only by the eyes.

It is a challenging act to outgrow sub-vocalising because:

- A lot of people have a reading ritual in terms of a prayer book or some other recital that they do from a book on a regular basis. They need to switch this habit of sub-vocalising on and off every time they change the reading matter. This keeps alive the sub-vocalising aspect somewhere inside their system, making it difficult to completely let it go.
- Sub-vocalising has a nasty tendency to return back if we let down our guard even for a little bit.

8 SHUTTING OUT DISTRACTIONS – LAUNCHING OFF TO SPEED

In The Boring Classrooms At School

While thinking of our early school years, we sometimes picture sitting inside a classroom and continuously having our attention focused on what the teacher was speaking, reading or writing. However, any slightest activity or movement inside or outside the classroom (it may be somebody passing by in the corridor or an insect, bird or animal in the vicinity of the classroom) would immediately catch the fancy of students (*Fig 8.1*). Somebody wanting to enter the classroom will be noticed immediately by every student in the class before the teacher.

Fig 8.1 Movement of butterfly distracting child

Movement is life, which is precisely the reason we would prefer watching a movie over reading a story any day. Incidentally, this is actually a defence mechanism provided to mankind in prehistoric times so that he could identify the slightest movement in his environment and protect himself from predators—other animals who would hurt or attack him. Though there are no predators around today, the reflex shift of gaze towards any moving object has remained with mankind even after centuries.

Reading And Lack Of Movement

When we're a reading a book, there is not much movement on the printed page. This leaves us at the risk of immediately looking at any moving object or even when there is none, our gaze keeps getting distracted. This takes our attention away from our track of reading.

Moving Ahead Or Back

Many people lose track of which line or paragraph they are on when reading. As a result, sometimes they skip a line or two or an entire paragraph. This is referred to as 'progression' (*Fig 8.2*). At other times, they end up re-reading the same line or paragraph. This is referred to as 'regression'.

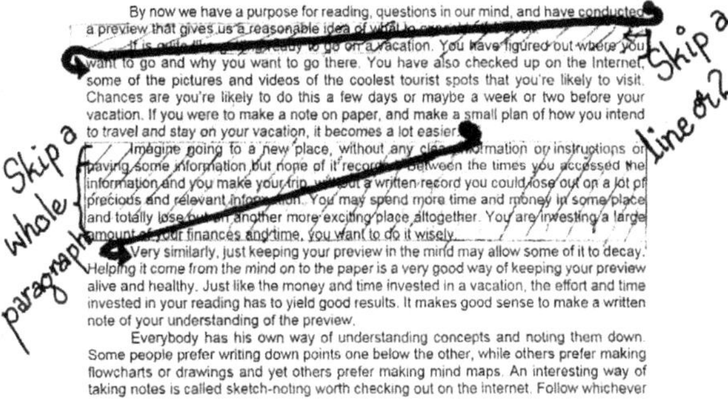

By now we have a purpose for reading, questions in our mind, and have conducted a preview that gives us a reasonable idea of [illegible]

It is [illegible] ready to go on a vacation. You have figured out where you want to go and why you want to go there. You have also checked up on the Internet, some of the pictures and videos of the coolest tourist spots that you're likely to visit. Chances are you're likely to do this a few days or maybe a week or two before your vacation. If you were to make a note on paper, and make a small plan of how you intend to travel and stay on your vacation, it becomes a lot easier.

Imagine going to a new place, without any [illegible]mation or instructions or having some information but none of it record[illegible] between the times you accessed the information and you make your trip [illegible] a written record you could lose out on a lot of precious and relevant info[illegible]. You may spend more time and money in some place and totally lose [illegible] another more exciting place altogether. You are investing a large amount [illegible] your finances and time, you want to do it wisely.

Very similarly, just keeping your preview in the mind may allow some of it to decay. Helping it come from the mind on to the paper is a very good way of keeping your preview alive and healthy. Just like the money and time invested in a vacation, the effort and time invested in your reading has to yield good results. It makes good sense to make a written note of your understanding of the preview.

Everybody has his own way of understanding concepts and noting them down. Some people prefer writing down points one below the other, while others prefer making flowcharts or drawings and yet others prefer making mind maps. An interesting way of taking notes is called sketch-noting worth checking out on the internet. Follow whichever

Fig 8.2 Skipping a line or paragraph while reading

Missing Reading-place Confuses Reader

If this progression or regression happens frequently, it can be quite frustrating as it results in slowing down of the reading, and also makes understanding of the matter more difficult. The brain tries to make sense from the small bits of information that is sent to it. When these bits are not in the right order, it fails to arrange them to get the bigger picture. For some people, this may be the reason of developing an aversion to reading.

Like A Jigsaw Puzzle

To an extent, reading can be compared to solving a jigsaw puzzle. If a proper system is followed, wherein, the border is made initially, and then gradually pieces of similar colour are provided followed by the placement of dissimilar colours in their respective places—it becomes easier to put the puzzle in place and eventually compose the whole picture.

However, if pieces are provided randomly and they do not fit with each other, an enjoyable task becomes laborious and cumbersome. This makes us lose out on the initial excitement.

Brain Wants The Whole Picture

The same logic applies when we begin to read. Our brain wants to make sense of the whole material that we read. But when we re-read the same material over and over again, the brain that is earlier longing to make sense of the whole picture gets restricted to just the first few lines or the beginning. This leads to boredom and also creates a hurdle in reaching the goal that is to see the whole picture.

The reason why our eyes move away from the actual direction of reading could be because of:

- slowed reading
- irregular eye movements
- easy distractibility
- daydreaming while reading

What is needed to deal with this is a tool that will—

1. keep our eyes on the line that we are reading on a continuous basis.
2. help us to increase our reading speed.
3. prevent any kind of distraction while reading.

A Launcher To The Rescue

It may come as a surprise to you that a simple blank 3"X4" card, which I refer to as a 'launcher' can serve all these three functions stated above. It helps you get the required speed, prevents unwanted distractions and continually, keeps you informed of where your reading line is.

This launcher derives its name from the launcher-rockets that are mostly used to propel a satellite out into space, away from the earth's gravitational pull (*Fig 8.3*). Once started these rockets cannot be stopped or slowed down and cannot return back. They have to pursue the decided course of direction and there's no scope of any change. The same principles apply to the launcher in case of reading.

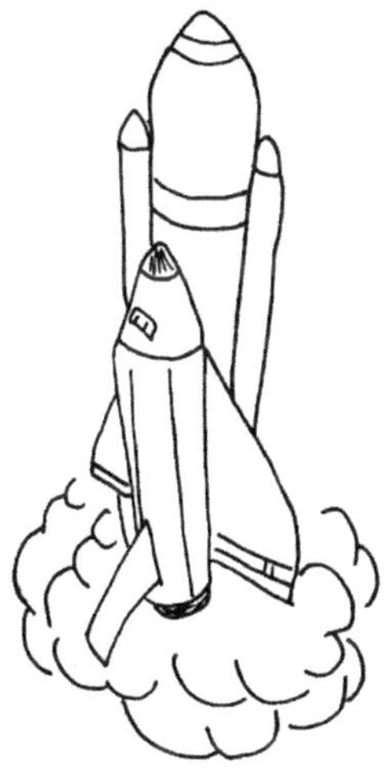

Fig 8.3 Rocket Launching

Rules Of Using A Launcher

This launcher has to be placed in a landscape manner at the centre of the printed column of the page (*Fig. 8.4*). It has to be placed above the line that you are about to read. This way you will read the lines below the launcher

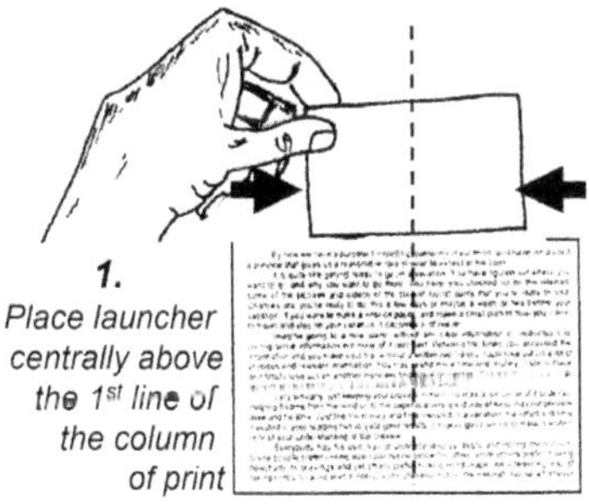

Fig 8.4 Placement of a Launcher

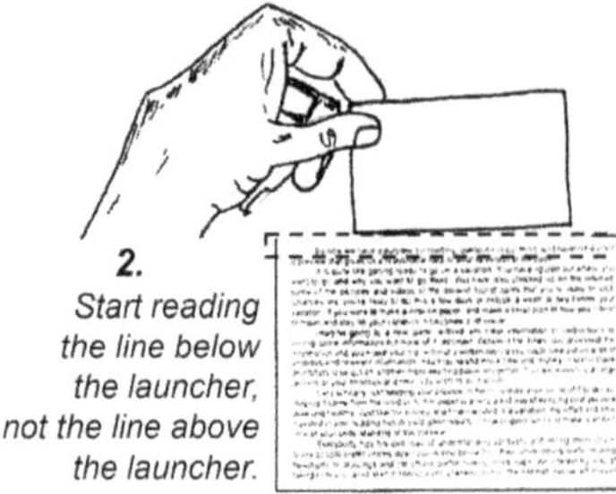

Fig 8.5 Reading the line below the launcher

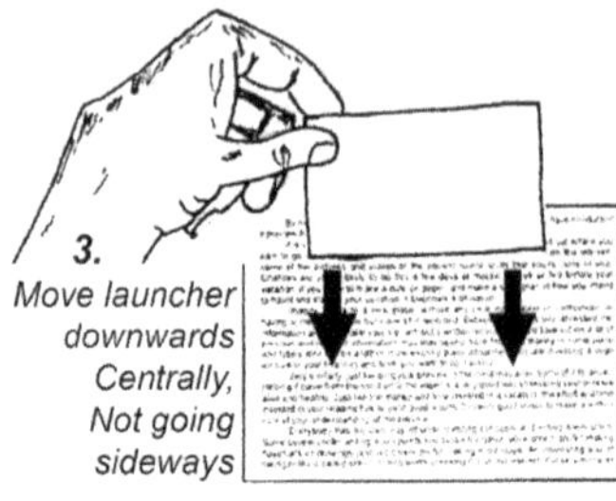

Fig 8.6 Move launcher downwards and not sideways

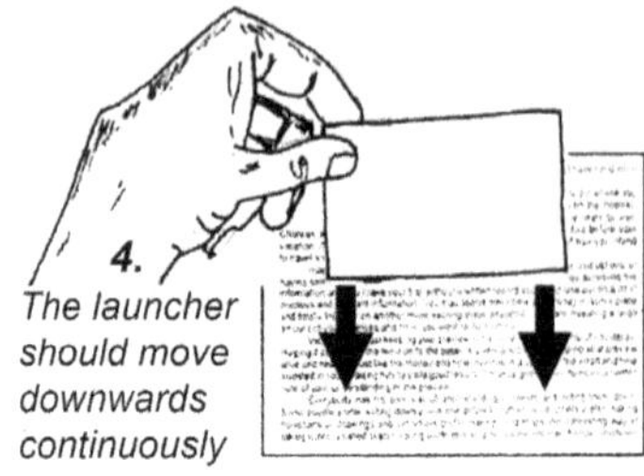

Fig 8.7 Moving launcher down continuously

(*Fig. 8.5*). You will now move the launcher down as you read every succeeding line (*Fig 8.6*). It has to be held with your left hand in such a way that your fingers do not obstruct the text you are reading.

Caution.

1. A launcher always moves from upward to downward direction, and not side to side (*Fig 8.7*).
2. At any point, the launcher cannot stop or go back upwards (*Fig 8.8*).

This way, your chances of getting lost on the line you are reading are minimised and regression is also prevented (*Fig 8.9*). Once you reach the bottom of the page, you move the launcher to the top of the next page and continue reading in the same way (*Fig 8.10*).

Brain's Response To The Launcher

Since it is a launcher, the orders given to the astronaut

Fig 8.8 Launcher cannot go upwards

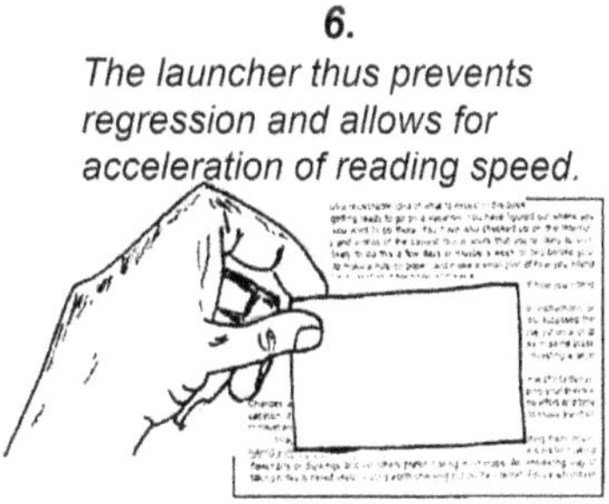

6.
The launcher thus prevents regression and allows for acceleration of reading speed.

Fig 8.9 Launcher prevents regression

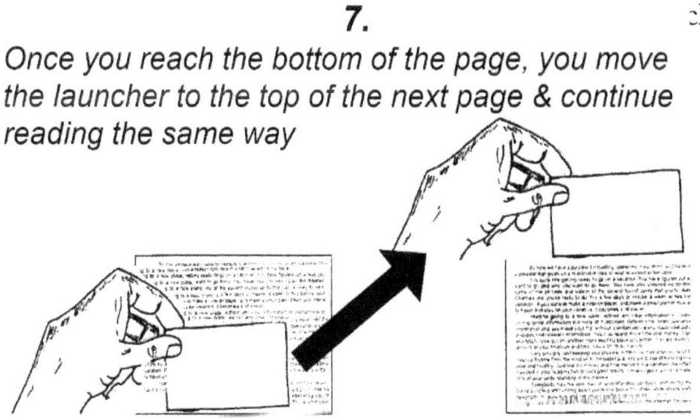

of the launcher (your brain) are very clear.

'No stopping.'

'No going back.'

When your brain knows clearly that you are only going to read the specific text once, and there will be no second chance to re-read the text—it becomes alert and focuses your eyes on what you're trying to read. This way your attention and therefore concentration is better, minimising the chances of distraction. When slowing down and going back are no options, the net speed of reading naturally increases. (If you are continuously going back to re-read, what you just read, you are obviously going ch slower

7.
Once you reach the bottom of the page, you move the launcher to the top of the next page & continue reading the same way

Fig 8.10 Shifting launcher from bottom of page to top of next page

Bonus Benefits Of Using A Launcher

There are various benefits of using a launcher.

Firstly, your eyes and brain experience less reading fatigue, so you feel fresh and are in a better position to acquire more speed.

Secondly, minus the re-reading and the resultant confusion, your understanding of the text that you are reading becomes easier. This enhances your interest, further acceleration your reading speed.

Beginner's Blues

Initially, using a launcher may feel a little awkward. But as the results will be immediate, you will be willing to continue despite the awkwardness. While the first fifteen minutes of using a launcher, it is not necessary to focus on increasing reading speed as much as it is important to get used to the feel of the launcher. With practice, as you start getting the hang of the launcher, you can gradually start increasing the speed of moving the launcher.

In the beginning, your eyes and brain may feel that you are being harsh on them, and they may even object by asking you, 'What do you think you're doing?' Though once this activity becomes a regular affair, just as it happens with increasing levels of a computer game, your eyes and brain will start taking up the challenge in a different light and get ready for the next level. Over some time, the initial difficulty will start easing out. Then you will be able to start reading at faster speeds, and the brain and eyes will prepare themselves for more challenges.

Thus, it is very important to tide over the initial awkwardness and to not give up easily.

The Neil Armstrong Way

Neil Armstrong had two near death experiences before he got selected to travel to the moon. *Had he decided to quit midway, would we have known him?* He had tremendous self-belief and faith in his mission which led him to glory. Similarly, your mission to take up reading in a better manner to enhance your life should be equally important to you. You don't want to end up as just another participant in the race, do you? You want to be a winner, don't you? Always remember—winners don't quit and quitters don't win.

Driving A Sports Car In Low Gears

Some people already use a launcher, but with a faulty technique. They read the line above the launcher. This is wrong because it exposes the lines they've just read, leaving the window open for regression or going back to a previous line. Also, by blocking the next line that they are about to read, they minimise their chances for acceleration, therefore, reading at a slower speed.

It is almost like driving a car focusing less on the windshield in front of you, and being obsessed with the rear view mirror that shows you the road that you have left behind. Now a driver, who continuously focuses on the road he has left behind will obviously drive slower than a driver who is focused on the road ahead, and thus, will be at a higher risk for accidents.

9 GETTING ACROSS QUICKLY – DON'T BE A COW, CHEW LESS

SMS For Slow Message Service

I know this may sound ridiculously stupid, but just for a moment think of what it would be like if the Short Messaging Service (SMS) could only send one word per message. In that case, if you had to convey a sentence to someone, you would probably have to send multiple SMSs so that the recipient would understand what you are trying to convey. While you are at it, can you imagine the amount of patience and tolerance it would demand from you to send it and from the recipient to receive and make sense of the message?

It is good to have the whole communication in one go. It makes understanding a whole lot easier task too. The same logic applies to our brain too when we're reading any text. If we send words at a slower pace, we test the patience of our very restless and information-hungry brain.

Maintaining A Good Scoring Rate

Reading can be compared to many popular sports around us. When your turn to perform comes, you have a target to be achieved. The longer you take to achieve it, the more difficult it becomes towards the closing stages of the game. The audience enjoys a fast-paced game just as much as the brain enjoys rapid inflow of information and consequent comprehension. The slower a player performs, the more daunting the task may appear and often the spectators give up any hope of a possible victory.

What is more is, if a player or a team, develops a reputation of doing things at their own slow-pace, though they may have a sound technique and may be a delight to watch—a very large proportion of the spectators may lose interest in the player, team, and sometimes even the sport. The audience wants action and they want it quick. Those who prefer slower-paced things are perhaps seated in a concert of classical music.

Brain Seeks Completion For Better Comprehension

When you are reading, the ultimate target for your brain is good and quick comprehension of the material read. The brain wants to make sense of the whole picture, and does not want to get stuck in partial details for too long. When reading is slow and consequent comprehension is difficult, it is no surprise that the reader eventually gets bored with the subject, and unfortunately, very often even with the entire act of reading.

Chasing A Target Score In Cricket

Let us take the example of a cricket match. The team batting second would prefer to chase down the score with a brisk run rate from the very beginning to avoid building up the pressure towards the latter part of the game. Runs can be scored in form of singles and twos, but any team would prefer getting them in fours and sixes. This is definitely a more efficient and less tiring way of accomplishing the target score. The present slow reading is similar to scoring runs in form of singles which tends to get boring after a certain amount of time. Also, it results in undue pressure.

Uninstructed Baseline Reading

We have already seen that at the time of reading if the eyes send one word during a single fixation, making four fixations per second—the reading speed gets restricted to 240 words per minute

(4 words/second X 60 seconds). We know that reading at less than the comprehension speed of the brain is an invitation to distraction and mind-wandering.

Increasing The Visual Bite

If however, at every fixation, we take two words instead of one—our reading speed becomes double, that is, 480 words per minute (2 words per fixation X 4 words/second X 60 seconds). If we assume the word processing ability of the brain to be about 500 words per minute, there is hardly any scope for distractions as the brain is satisfactorily occupied with the new incoming information. Similarly, if we take three words per fixation, our reading speed would become triple, which would be 720 words per minute.

But so far, throughout our life, we have only been taking in one word per fixation. Right?

No, this is absolutely wrong!!!

Remember the few hours, just before exams, when you had loads to read, but very little time at hand? You were reading at much higher speeds, taking in multiple words per fixation at that moment. Your confidence of what you were reading was also sky high; more out of necessity then out of comfort.

This Cannot Be Done Regularly

I can already sense a slight negativity in your thinking as you discard those moments as being *nothing much* or *not really serious*. Our main difficulty here is that we do not trust our eyes or our brain when we start reading at a faster pace. Let us look at what our eyes can see in a fixation.

Central and peripheral vision. Our visual field (the entire spectrum of what you can see when you look straight) has two components—the central vision and the peripheral vision.

Central vision refers to whatever comes in your main focus when you are looking straight ahead, while peripheral vision refers to everything else in the surrounding that you can see, but may not be focusing on at that particular moment.

Though you may be focusing on your central vision, you are also distinctly aware of your other surroundings. While you're reading a book, you're definitely aware of somebody who has entered the room and though you may not shift your gaze from your book, you know where the person has eventually settled in the room or if that person has moved out of the room. You can notice all this movement because of your peripheral vision.

The irony of peripheral vision. We rely on our central vision mostly for the things that need our focused attention like reading, stitching, cooking, etc. But *how much do we trust our peripheral vision?*

Well… a whole lot!

And paradoxically, not much!

A whole lot. We trust our peripheral vision even when lives are at stake. For instance, when we are driving a vehicle, we keep our head focused straight ahead. We trust what we see through our peripheral vision, seldom moving our head to assess people, vehicles, or other traffic that may cross us perpendicularly.

Not at all. When it comes to reading words on a harmless line of print, we freeze and are reluctant to delegate any responsibility to our peripheral vision. The bottom line is, the moment we can start taking in more words per fixation, we are on our way to a much quicker and better way of reading. At that time, we just cannot trust the peripheral vision.

Your Present Visual Bite

On an average, a column of print has around twelve words per line. At the previous rate of slow reading and reading one word per fixation, we would make twelve fixations and thirteen saccades per line of print. That would amount to around additional four seconds per line, as we can only make four saccades or less per second.

Fig 9.1 Take a single sheet of A4 Transparency (Acetate Sheet)

Increasing your visual bite. Our objective is to move across the line of print in such a way that we move across the entire line in four saccades, taking only one second per line of print. Let us now look at how to take in more words per fixation.

Logic. We will only be making four fixations per line. While we fixate our eyes on each of these words, we are also able to see the words on the right and the left of these words.

Challenge. Now this poses a challenge to trust the brain to receive and process even those words that were not fixated upon.

Method. To make just four fixations per second, one option is to count the words on the line and number them so that we can stop **only** on the second, fifth, eight and eleventh word on every line.

Problem. Counting words can again slow us down and dissolve the entire purpose of reaching up to a good reading speed. What is needed here is a system of dividing the column of reading text by an indication that helps us make just four stops per page.

Solution. The best solution is to use longitudes, which is a transparent sheet with four equally spaced vertical parallel lines running from top to bottom.

The making of a longitudes sheet. Take an A4 size transparency, also known as acetate sheet (*Fig. 9.1 and 9.2*). Place it in a landscape

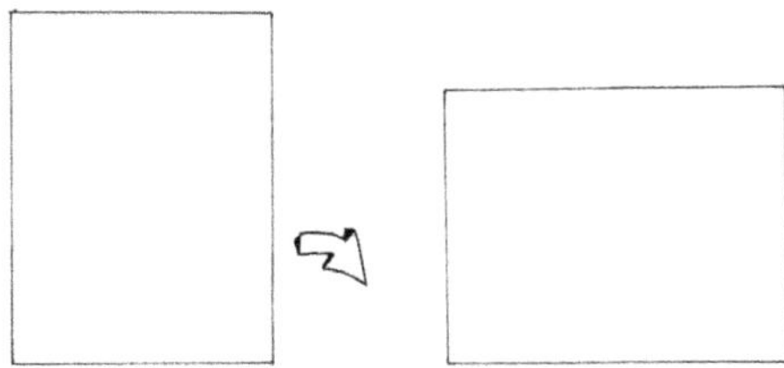

Fig 9.2 Place transparency in landscape manner

manner (*Fig. 9.3*) and divide it into two equal parts (*Fig. 9.4*) by means of a vertical line drawn in the middle of the sheet, running from top to bottom. Take any one of these sheets which now appear to be placed in a portrait fashion. On this sheet, using a thin OHP marker, draw four equally spaced parallel lines running from top to bottom, so that the transparency is divided into five rectangles of equal area (*Fig. 9.5*). This is your longitudes sheet, hereafter referred to as the 'longitudes' (*Fig. 9.6*).

Placement of longitudes. Place this longitudes sheet centrally on the printed page (column of reading text) such that the lines marked

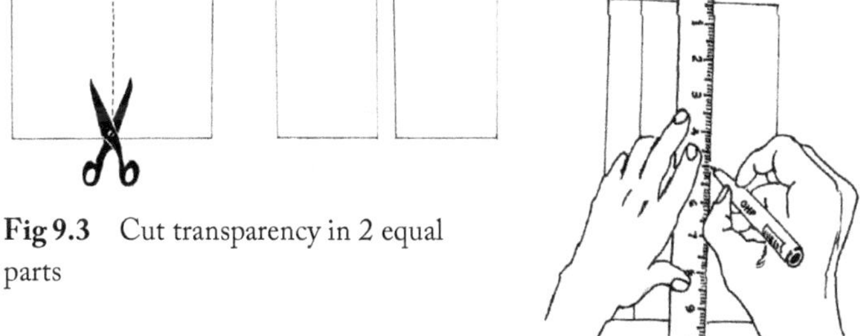

Fig 9.3 Cut transparency in 2 equal parts

Fig 9.4 Draw 4 equally spaced vertical parallel lines on transparency using OHP marker

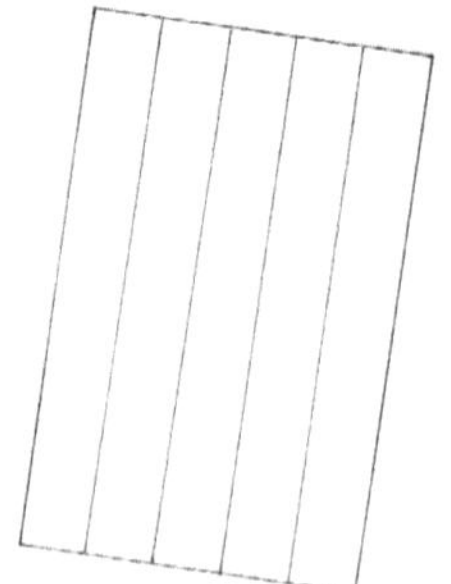

Fig 9.5 A Ready Longitude Sheet

Fig 9.6 Longitude placement centrally on reading column

with OHP marker run parallel to the vertical margins and the central binding on the page (*Fig. 9.7*). These lines of OHP should be perpendicular to the lines of print that you are about to read.

Using the longitudes. Once the longitudes are in place, you need to change your method of reading by not stopping at every printed word on the line. You should only let your eyes stop on those words that are intercepted by the longitudes. This way, you start reading the first line of the page with that word which is intercepted by the vertical longitude and move to the next word that is intercepted by the next longitude (and not the next word to the immediate right).

Moving across quicker. When you start reading in this manner—you keep moving across the line, stopping only at those words which are intercepted by the longitudes while deliberately omitting those words that are not intercepted by the longitudes. So, this means that you stop your eyes on the first longitude and then instead of going to the next word, you take your eyes to the word on the same line below the next longitude and then to the third longitude and so on.

Reducing Fixations Per Line

Effectively instead of fixating on twelve or thirteen words per line, your eyes will now be fixating only on those four words that are being intercepted by the longitudes. But they will still be reading all the twelve or thirteen words (even if you don't believe it yet). This way, even though your eyes will fixate only on four words as they move, they will be receptive to all the words on the line. Once you reach the end of the line, you move to the next line on to the word that is intercepted by the first longitude.

Feeling Lost Is Allowed Initially

It is natural to feel lost initially and have no sense of comprehension whatsoever for the first few minutes. Though as you persist with this technique, a surprising phenomenon occurs. You would realise that even when you are not reading every word, over time, you do seem to understand what you are reading.

What Actually Happens

What happens here is that you stopped your eyes on the second, fifth, eighth and eleventh word on each line. Now, while your eyes focused on these words, they could also see part or whole of the adjacent words on the left as well as on the right. For example, when you fixated on the second word, your eyes could read part or whole of the first and the third word as well. Similarly, when your eyes fixated on the fifth word, they could see the fourth and the sixth word as well. Thus, you read and comprehend the entire line while only stopping at four words.

Comprehension Soon Catches Up In Spite Of Doubts

When you have just started using this technique, you may have a lot of doubts in your mind about its efficacy. However, as you go on practising this, and as you pick up the speed, your comprehension also quickly catches up. Not only does this helps you to move through lines, paragraphs and pages quicker, but it also reduces the fatigue and tiredness experienced by the tiny muscles that move the eyeball. What we are trying to achieve here is quick movement of the eyes across the line of print from left to right.

Customise Your Longitudes If You Wish To

You may start out with the longitudes that we have recommended or you may use a customised longitudes sheet that you have prepared as per your needs. To begin with, your lines may have lesser space between them and can be more in number. Then as you garner enough confidence, you can increase the space between these lines. So initially, there may be about five lines and as your confidence increases, you can make it just four lines or three lines as you get comfortable with the technique.

But Our Brain's Processing Speed Is Only...

Some readers must be wondering while using the longitudes, we are sending three words per fixation at the rate of four fixations per second. This means, there are 720 words being sent to the brain per minute. But you were just told that our brain's processing ability is approximately 500 words per minute. *Then how does the brain manage to process the extra 220 words per minute?*

Just like the brain adjusts to increasing speeds and more complex levels in case of a video/computer game, similarly it manages to process the extra words that reaches it. Observe that when we begin to play a new game, the brain finds the rules and controls quite complex to understand initially. It's only with time and practice that the eye-brain-hand co-ordination catches up and we are able to adapt to more complex levels in the game—as if the brain develops those extra muscles to cope with increasing demands. In fact, not only does it cope, it starts relishing and enjoying the challenge that comes in its way. Once it has reached that level of word processing, it doesn't have any difficulty starting again at that speed and is ready to build more brain muscle for higher word processing.

Save Time and Energy, Protect Your Brain

Not only do these activities save time while reading, but they also rejuvenate our neurons. Thereby helping us develop more brain connections or 'synapses' through a process called 'neuroplasticity', which has neuro-protective capabilities against illnesses like depression, anxiety and dementia.

10 SPEED KILLS DISTRACTIONS – JUST READ FAST

Do all of us have a natural walking speed? Do we all continue walking at that natural speed all the time? Of course not!

Fig 10.1 Leisurely Stroll along beachside

When we're strolling along a beachside with our family, we take all our steps at a leisurely pace, allowing the waves from the ocean to lash against our feet (*Fig 10.1*). On the contrary, when you're late for an important meeting, you take hasty big steps, rushing towards your destination to try and still reach in time (*Fig 10.2*).

Similarly, if you are a slow reader, your reading is like the stroll along the beach. You take your own time to get through the reading material. This was an excellent way to read during the early reading years. Back then, we were still learning how to pronounce words, and were in the process of acquiring and developing a vocabulary bank.

Fig 10.2 When late for a meeting

Vocabulary Has Grown, Why Shouldn't We Too?

Presently if you are above twelve years of age, your vocabulary has multiplied several times with what it was when you first started out. There are three possible reasons why we may still be reading slowly:

1. The apprehension of coming across unfamiliar words keeps as scared of reading fast.
2. Our belief that if we go fast, we may miss out on a few words that may be important and therefore miss out on the exact meaning of whatever we are attempting to read.
3. Our long-held notion that for better comprehension, we need to read slowly and carefully.

Why These Three Notions Are Actually Misconceptions?

If you are reading a subject that you are acquainted with, your frequency of coming across unfamiliar words is limited. Also, if you do come across unfamiliar words, they won't be one after the other in the same paragraph, but will probably be further apart. In this case, you can easily avoid reading at a slower speed.

Our brain thrives on the concept of the whole. Whenever it is presented with an image, a sentence, a task, or a situation, that is unfinished or incomplete, it immediately gets to work and tries to see what it would look like in its complete 'finished' form. Let me illustrate this with an example: (*Fig.10.3*)

Fig 10.3 The triangle that never was

What do you see in the figure illustrated above?

Most people will observe it to be three incomplete circles with a triangle placed between them. Geometrically speaking, none of those is a complete circle or a triangle. Yet, these missing gaps are quickly filled up by our brain to give us the completed geometric forms.

Here is yet another very popular optical illusion. You can see two figures here (*Fig 10.4*).

On the left is a man blowing a trumpet. The image on the right appears to be a girl's face. The first one is a mere shadow and the second one barely shows any details. Yet, what is missing in both the images is filled up by our magnificent brain. As if this is not enough, some people may even go to the extent of describing the mood of both these characters.

Fig 10.4 Man blowing a trumpet

Auto-predict Feature Of Brain

This same logic is valid and true for language as well. Very often when you're watching a movie, the characters say something and pause—during which time you have already predicted what the character is likely to say. More often than not you are somewhat right in your prediction.

Does this still not appeal to you and do you still question the applicability of this concept in reading?

Can You Read This?

Olny srmat poelpe can. I Cdnuolt blveiee taht I cluod aulaclty uesdnatnrd waht I was rdanieg. The phaonmneal pweor of the hmuan mnid, aoccdrnig to a rscheearch at Cmabrigde Uinervtisy syas—it deosn't mttaer in waht oredr the ltteers in a wrod are, the olny iprmoatnt thing is taht the frist and lsat ltteer be in the rghit pclae. The rset can be a taotl mses and you can sitll raed it woulndt be a porbelm. This is bcuseae the huamn mnid deos not raed ervey lteter by istlef, but the wrod as a wlohe.

Amzanig huh? yaeh and I awlyas tghuhot slpeling was ipmorantt!

Of Course You Read It and Here's Why:

When you must have started reading this, you may have had a slight difficulty in the first few words. However, your brain must have quickly adjusted to the incorrect spellings in the words, and by the time you reached the second line, you were comfortable and quicker in reading the words correctly. Towards the end of the paragraph, you must be almost reading it at your regular reading speed.

Your brain not only automatically corrects mistakes; it also fills in gaps which the author may have left out. This way, you end up automatically eliminating minor mistakes so that the complete sentence be read properly (*Fig 10.5*).

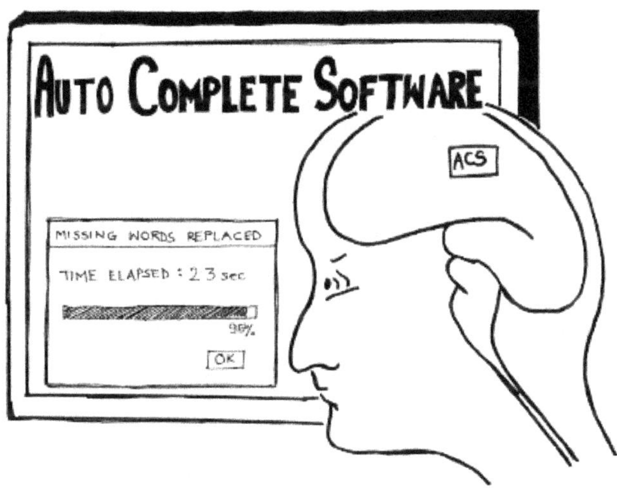

Fig 10.5 Auto complete software of brain

You Always Want More Proofs, Don't You?

Below this line is a triangle which has a few words inside it (*Fig 10.6*). Do not read them. Instead, cover the triangle with a card.

Now, with the flick of the wrist, just uncover the triangle for a flash of a second. Could you read it? If you did, fine. If you did not, repeat the exercise once more. What did you read?

Fig 10.6 Triangle of I love Paris

Did you read—'I love Paris in the springtime?'

If you did, you are one of a majority, that is you can count yourself with 95 per cent of the total population who can read English. Now, may I please request you to repeat the exercise one last time?

This time remove the card, and slowly and carefully read what it says in the triangle. It says, 'I love Paris in the the springtime.' Though the article *the* was printed twice, our brain conveniently overlooked it.

Off With The Trash

Our brain has this amazing ability to filter out what may be unnecessary and irrelevant so that only the appropriate is read out. When you read fast, your brain is not only filtering out the unnecessary, it is also predicting the next words. It is somewhat like the auto-completion feature in some word-processing software; similar to a latest feature of mobile phones that predicts the remainder of the word when you are typing a short message (SMS) or the name of a contact in your contact's list.

Trust Your Brain

Therefore, when you're reading, you have to trust your brain to be able to make sense even from a few words, and not necessarily wait to read all the words to understand the meaning. It is not very important to get into the nitty-gritty details of the language like spellings and punctuation, so long as we can understand what the writer is trying to convey.

The only exception can be a proof-reader—who has to ensure that these kind of grammatical lapses do not go unnoticed. For the other 99.99% of readers, just accelerate your reading speed.

Don't Stop, The Journey Ahead Will Clarify

When reading, the brain wants to understand the whole picture and not just parts of it. So often, it happens that when a reader finds a concept difficult, he tends to get stuck in re-reading the same content in the hope of better understanding. This is actually an ineffective and unproductive method of reading. If the reader continued to read the chapter or content ahead, what was not understood earlier could become easier to understand in the further paragraphs.

Invitation To A Movic

Let us look at an analogy to understand how our brain functions.

I invite a class of hundred students to a free private screening of a latest much awaited film in a rented mini theatre at 3 p.m., meant exclusively for them. Seventy students arrive at the theatre before time and seat themselves, and we start the movie sharp at 3 p.m. as instructed. At 3.10 p.m., we are joined by another ten students who request to restart the movie. After asking for the consent of those who had previously assembled, we restart the movie from the very beginning at 3.15 p.m.

Now, the first group of seventy who arrived before time are not pleased with the re-run of the beginning, but out of respect for me, they permit it.

Another five minutes later—at 3.20 p.m., the last batch of twenty students, who are all girls reach the theatre. They announce their arrival with loud screams of—'sir please restart, sir please!!!' There is no scope for discussion or argument when a chorus of pleading young girls make a vociferous request. So we restart the movie a second time at 3.25 p.m.

While the second batch of ten students cannot protest, the first batch of seventy students are pretty annoyed at having to see the same beginning a third time. They now begin to lose interest in the same movie that they were earlier watching with great excitement. Their brains get fed up.

Same is the case with reading. Once you have started a chapter, just keep moving on and on till you reach the end of the chapter. If you keep reading a paragraph several times in the hope of a better understanding, you may end up damaging your interest and enthusiasm in reading it. It will make you feel demotivated and you will end up with no progression with the chapter. You will then decide to attempt to read it later when you will be in the mood for it or better prepared. That way, you will successfully procrastinate and delay something that could be accomplished at that particular moment. It will now be added to your to-do-list as well as be a cause for stress.

Had you continued reading the chapter, chances are high that you would have made sense of what was difficult earlier through the subsequent explanations and clarifications in the chapter.

Read For The Gist

It is important to note that it is practically impossible to remember everything you read. However you must read for just the gist of the content (*Fig 10.7*). As books cannot be written in short forms or telegraphic language, authors are compelled to add a lot more words as fillers to make their content coherent and sensible. All of the fillers need not be remembered.

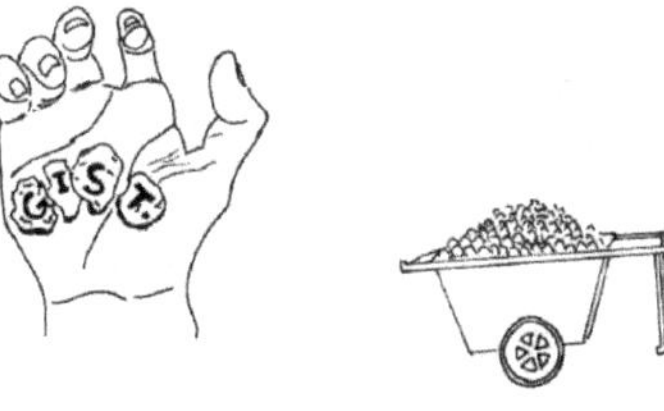

Fig 10.7 Read for the gist

Gist is the King. Purpose, persistence and progression are keys to better reading.

11 EMBOLDENING CONFIDENCE – INCREASING VOCABULARY ADDS POWER

Familiarity Enhances Confidence

Let's say you have stayed in a city for the more than five to six years. You are bound to know the streets as well as the landmarks and the various routes therein. Compared to a tourist who is new to the city and keeps asking for landmarks to get to one place from another, you will have significantly less difficulty in navigating around the city. Someone who has been driving a taxi cab in the same city for the same number of years as you will be definitely better versed than both you and the tourist when it comes to moving around in the city. This can be attributed to 'familiarity' and 'repeated exposure'.

The same logic applies to reading.

If you are a frequent reader, your vocabulary will be definitely more than that of a non-reader. If you are a non-reader and have taken to reading now, over time, your vocabulary will improve tremendously compared to what it was when you were a non-reader. So once you become familiar with the basic vocabulary and are willing to add on to it, gradually your confidence will enhance and you will become a better reader.

Vocabulary Enhances Processing

Without any training in 'reading enhancement', your brain is capable of processing more than 500 words per minute. Let's be honest, the brain will only process the words that it knows. Simply put, the better your vocabulary, the quicker your processing of words. Hence, your confidence in reading quickly will also increase once your vocabulary enhances.

Building Vocabulary Is An Ongoing Process

Vocabulary-building is a continuous process, it goes on throughout your life (*Fig 11.1*). The gain in your vocabulary will depend largely on your reading habit as well as your exposure to the language in terms of who you interact with and what you are exposed to internet, television and other media. A rough graph to show what the average progress of vocabulary over ages looks like is illustrated below.

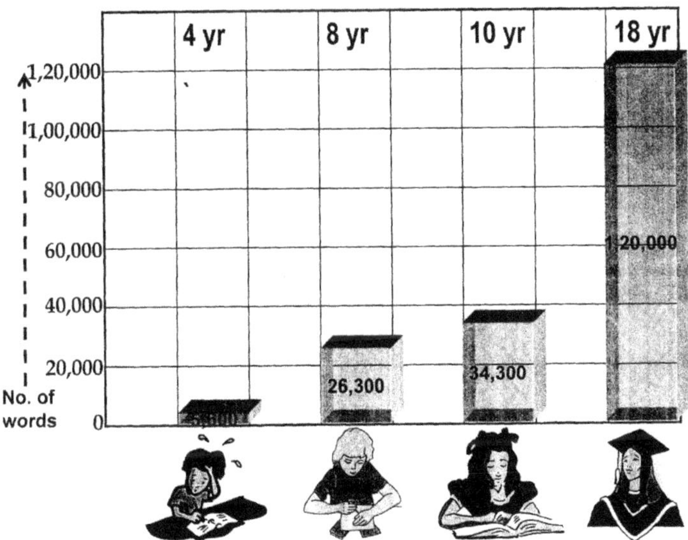

Fig 11.1 Increasing Vocabulary with Age

Words are symbols for ideas. These ideas formulate knowledge and knowledge is gained mostly through words. Each subject has its own vocabulary and is like a new language when you first come to it.

Vocabulary building books. There are two books that you could use to add value to your vocabulary. You should keep them handy at all times. The first is a **dictionary** and the next is a **thesaurus.** The dictionary, as we all know gives us the meanings of words and the manner in which they should be pronounced. The thesaurus is a reference book that has words with similar meanings which can be used alternatively (*Fig 11.2*).

great [greyt]

Main Entry: great
Part of Speech: adjective
Definition: very large
Synonyms: abundant, ample, big, big league, bulky, bull, colossal, considerable, decided, enormous, excessive, extended, extensive, extravagant, extreme, fat, gigantic, grievous, high, huge, humongous, husky, immense, inordinate, jumbo, lengthy, long, major league, mammoth, mondo, numerous, oversize, prodigious, prolonged, pronounced, protracted, strong, stupendous, terrible, titanic, towering, tremendous, vast, voluminous
Antonyms: few, little, miniature, minute, short, small

THESAURUS

Dictionary

great

[greyt]

adjective, **greater, greatest.**

1. unusually or comparatively large in size or dimensions:
   A great fire destroyed nearly half the city
2. large in number; numerous:
   Great hordes of tourists descend on Europe each summer

Fig 11.2 A Thesaurus & a Dictionary

If you do not already have these books for any reason, I strongly recommend you visit a book store and make this important investment right away. My suggestion is—do not go in for books that have more words in too fine or small print. You are better off with a book that has lesser words, but a more readable print (font) size. This will ensure less strain on your eyes and increase the chances of referring to it more often.

Computers in vocabulary building. Those of you who always have access to a computer (although, I don't recommend you should have one for it is a continuous source of distraction), can use the inbuilt thesaurus in the word processor software. In Microsoft Office, the shortcut keys for accessing the thesaurus are **Shift + F7.**

Move On, Refer Later

When you come across a word that you are not familiar with in the text, it makes sense to just underline it for that moment, and not stop your reading to look for its meaning in a reference book. As you read the rest of the line/paragraph/chapter, the meaning of that word may become clear to you without having to check. It is only after you have finished all your reading for the session, that you should reach out for the reference books and verify your understanding of the words. This way your reading rhythm will not get broken, and speed and comprehension of your reading will also be maintained.

Notebook For New Words

It may help to have some kind of a handy notebook in which you may maintain a list of unfamiliar words and as you finish reading a particular assignment, you should record all your unfamiliar words in this notebook. When it is convenient, look these words up in the dictionary. It may be a good idea to record their meanings as well in the notebook. This will reinforce the new word into your vocabulary and for any reason, if it slips your mind, one more glance at the word in the notebook will etch it onto your brain forever.

A Word For A Word Makes You Rise And Wise

This adds to your confidence and command over the language. You are now a person who takes pride in enhancing his language skills. At times, when looking up the meaning of one word, you will need to look up a second word and a third, or a string of words. Your brain may just relish this exercise as you end up learning five words where you started to learn just one new word. As you do this, it keeps on getting easier and you start enjoying yourself.

Little Research, Big Promotion

It also helps to familiarise yourself with prefixes, suffixes and roots (*Fig 11.3*) (words taken from other languages, especially from Latin, occasionally French and Greek). Knowing the meanings and the applications of these prefixes, suffixes and roots enhances your familiarity with even more new words, and adds to your reading confidence and speed. After a while, you may even start guessing the meanings of new words as you come across them, and you will be surprised to find that you are right mostly.

Fig 11.3 Roots of Words

One New Word A Day, Keeps Ignorance Astray

I will recommend Norman Lewis's *Instant Word Power* as a good tool in this regard. Most newspapers and magazines often give out a new word for the day, explain what it means and how it can be used. Even referring and adding one or two new words to your vocabulary can go a long way in adding to your confidence of the language.

It may not be right to say that vocabulary adds to one's self-esteem, but at the same time it won't be wrong to say that lack

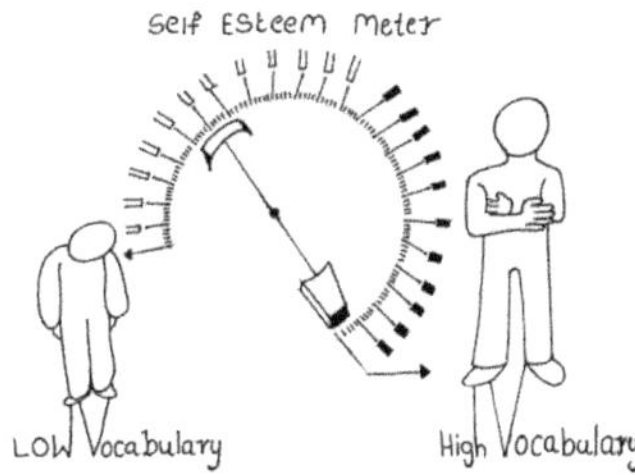

Fig 11.4 Vocabulary and Self Esteem

of a good vocabulary has often dented the self-esteem of many of the aspiring students and professionals alike (*Fig11.4*).

Know The Route, Speed Away

Without a good vocabulary, reading is like driving a huge trailer truck with manual stick shift (gears) lacking power steering in an unfamiliar territory with narrow lanes and frequent turnings. You have to continuously stop and start. Possessing a good vocabulary makes reading feel like driving an automatic transmission sports car on an airport runway.

12 BELIEVING IN SELF – COMPREHENSION WILL CATCH UP

The Victor

by: C. W. Longenecker

If you think you are beaten, you are.
If you think you dare not, you don't.
If you like to win but think you can't,
It's almost a cinch you won't.
If you think you'll lose, you're lost.
For out in the world we find
Success begins with a fellow's will.
It's all in the state of mind.
If you think you are out classed, you are.
You've got to think high to rise.
You've got to be sure of your-self before
You can ever win the prize.
Life's battles don't always go
To the stronger or faster man.
But sooner or later, the man who wins
Is the man who thinks he can.

This poem holds good for many aspects of life, but most strongly it is true for reading. Unfortunately, at a very early phase in childhood, certain experiences make an aspiring learner develop a negative outlook towards reading. Whatever reading they do for the rest of their life, is more to just get through their life rather than to get ahead.

Fig 12.1 Student ridiculed by a teacher

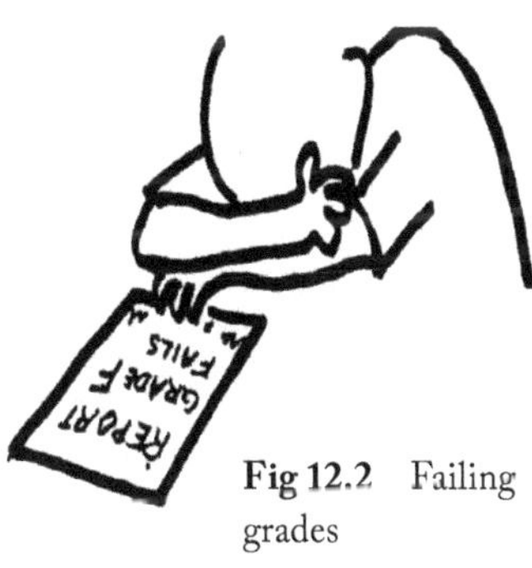

Fig 12.2 Failing grades

Being ridiculed by a teacher (*Fig 12.1*), not faring well in a particular subject (*Fig 12.2*), somebody being slightly better than you at reading—are just some of the many unacknowledged events that go a long way in pushing a person farther away from reading with a passion. Over time, these events get forgotten.

Without any serious thought, we assume our lack of initiative in reading to be an unchangeable part of our personality.

As You Think, So Shall You Be

Fig 12.3 Thoughts make a person

Our thinking plays a very crucial role in deciding the course of our life (*Fig 12.3*). Our thoughts become our beliefs. Our beliefs become our actions. Our actions then become our habits. We all know the benefits of good habits and yet we can't change them often because our efforts in the past were met with lots of resistance and difficulties. We give up easily convincing ourselves that even with our present system, we are living our life. *Then why make that extra effort and get through unnecessary inconvenience?*

With a little modification of the first stanza, it would still apply just as well and read as:

If you think you are past reading, you are.
If you think you care not to read, you don't.
If you like to read, but think you can't,
It's almost a cinch you won't.

So to get back to 'enhanced reading' ways, we need to do some introspection on our thoughts concerning reading and belief in ourselves.

As If Others Know Best

Often, we find ourselves inclined to give other people, and their thoughts and beliefs more importance than we do to our own thoughts and beliefs (*Fig 12.4*). Which is why, children will often change whatever topic they were reading before an exam, when they see their friends reading some other topic. Somehow it appears to them that their friend is better or knows more about what is right than they themselves do. This stems largely from low self-esteem and lack of self-belief.

Fig 12.4 Increase Self Belief

Low Self-Belief

As if the world doesn't do enough to dent our self-belief, we embark on this self-mutilating habit—almost ignorantly and unconsciously. We always feel we are less than others, especially when it comes to reading. Though you have read something just now, but when asked how well you know or have understood what you just read, most of you would prefer to be given one more chance to go through the same text before being quizzed. This self-doubting has a major impact on our comprehension of the material that we read.

A Matter Of Perception And Reassessment

This assumed negative perception should be challenged at the earliest. When proof to the contrary is provided, it becomes possible to start believing more positively in your own ability to comprehend. It could be in the form of a friend, teacher, activity, workshop or a book, which makes the person reassess the actual ability to understand the read material and to give up on all the previously-held negative notions.

Unfortunately, a very minute percentage of population gets access to such a vital awakening. For most of the other people, this wrongly held assessment of their lesser ability to understand the read material is etched in their minds.

In Our Reading Enhancement Workshops

Let me share my experience of having conducted workshops on reading enhancement. When I gave the participants a passage to read and followed it up with ten questions to be answered, I discovered this underrating of one's own comprehension unfailingly time and again. After the first passage and its comprehension, when participants were asked to estimate how many answers they would have gotten right, more than ninety per cent of participants gave a guess that was less than what they actually got right.

They were then compelled to read the next passage at a much faster pace, not worrying about how much they would understand. When they read at speeds increased by thirty to fifty per cent, they were themselves amazed at how their comprehension skills had actually shot up. This would go a long way in reinforcing their faith in their own comprehension ability as I was warmly informed through communication received from participants, months and sometimes even years after their participation in workshops.

Value Your Abilities More

When asked about your ability in any sphere of life, always give a positive response. Having done this, you will be amazed at how all your human faculties will work hard to try and live up to your expectations. If on the other hand, you give a below average response about your level of skill to any ability, your body faculties will drop down to that poor level that you uttered in your low confidence.

The Entrepreneur Henry Ford

Henry Ford so rightly said, 'Whether you think you can or whether you think you can't, you're right.' He very truly emphasised on the power of 'thinking' over 'ability'. Most readers give up on reading early because they perceive their comprehension ability to be inferior than others. Once they start having doubts over their comprehension ability, negative thoughts and events make them believe that their ability to understand is not much reliable.

Blessed With The Faculty Of Choice

As humans, we are blessed with an intellect and the faculty of choice. We can choose a more positive opinion of our abilities or continue to hold onto our previously-held negative perceptions. Our choice would make all the difference.

As a psychiatrist, I understand many people would rate themselves low, so that if their performance was lower, they would not have to face criticism or ridicule from others because they had rated themselves higher. They do not realise that in continuously having a low opinion of own ability, they are depriving themselves of many opportunities for a better life ahead.

Believe In Yourself, You Deserve To

Now before you attempt to read any material, tell yourself in your mind and mean it, 'I believe in my reading ability and so I am going to clearly understand and remember what I am about to read.' Just saying this has a very positive and uplifting impact on your senses and attention-paying ability. When this is combined with the added concentration provided by the launcher, and a good reading speed—there is no scope for distraction or reduced comprehension.

So go ahead and believe in yourself. Your God given abilities need to be acknowledged.

13 REGULAR PRACTICE – SHARPENS SKILL, AUTHORITATIVE FEEL

Bad News, Good News

From being a non-reader to having reached this page in the book, I must compliment you for the initiative shown. Although I am happy to have you with me this far ahead in the book, I must share some bad news. Whatever reading skills you have acquired from this book thus far are temporary and could be lost soon. Don't be disheartened. Hold on, there's a good news too.

The good news is that there is a way out. Using what you have acquired thus far diligently on a regular basis will ensure that this newly acquired skill becomes an ingrained part of you.

The magic word is **practice**.

We normally associate practice with performers, mostly sportspersons, actors and professionals like engineers, doctors and accountants. When we see any of these people not performing to their full potential, we are quick to attribute this to their lack of exposure, experience or practice.

Awareness Of Competence

We normally learn something new and then practice it till it becomes easier for us to do in our routine life. There are various levels of increasing competence that one gains with exposure and time.

The four stages are:

1. Unconscious incompetence
2. Conscious incompetence
3. Conscious competence
4. Unconscious competence

I'm not trying to expose you to some psychological jargons here. When you understand these levels of competence, you will be able to master your frustrations for any new learning you do in life.

Let us look at these stages with an example.

Unconscious incompetence. A small five-year-old looks at an older sibling riding a bicycle for the first time. The child throws a tantrum and asks to be given an opportunity to ride the same bike. When he sees the older sibling having fun on the bike, he assumes it is easy for him to do the same.

Fig 13.1 Unconscious Incompetence

This is the stage of 'unconscious incompetence' (*Fig 13.1*). It means that he is unaware that he cannot do this. His parents tell him it is risky and that he may hurt himself because he does not know how to ride a bicycle and he may fall. This is also similar to what many viewers feel when watching a talent show on television. What the performer is doing doesn't look so great and it feels, as if it could be easily replicated.

Conscious incompetence. Child insists that he be left alone on the bicycle to ride it by himself. The reluctant parent lets go and the child barely moves ahead and has a fall. This is the stage of 'conscious incompetence' (*Fig 13.2*). The child is now aware

Fig 13.2 Conscious Incompetence

(conscious) of his inability to ride (incompetence) the bicycle. The same would happen if you attempt to do at home what the performer does on television. You would certainly become aware of your inability to do something that looks so easy on television.

Conscious competence. The child is hurt and angry at having lost his balance and fallen. Now, out of sheer rivalry as well as jealousy because of what his sibling can do, he resolves to learn to ride the bicycle himself. After all, why should the sibling only have so much fun? Over time, and with many more falls, the child finally learns to ride a bicycle. This is the stage of 'conscious competence' (*Fig 13.3*). The child knows (conscious) he can ride the bicycle (competence). It takes a while for him to stabilise himself and get going on the bicycle. He has to focus while he rides the bicycle.

Fig 13.3 Conscious Incompetence

You resolve to learn, and try and master what you see on television. Over a period of time, you will find yourself being able to do the same. It may not be at the same level at which the performer on television was doing, but you have learned to do it. This gives you a sense of tremendous satisfaction and releases happy hormones (endorphins) in your body which make you feel exceptionally good.

Unconscious competence. It has been a few months since the child has been riding the bicycle. Now, he need not worry about sitting correctly on the seat or striking a very delicate balance while on the bicycle. He can even get someone else to sit with him and still be able to balance the bicycle. There are times when in an effort to show off, he may leave one or both the hands while cycling. He doesn't even think (unconscious) or focus about his effort of bicycling (competence). He is thinking of the next thing he needs to do once he gets to where he is planning to reach. This is the fourth stage or learning referred to as the stage of 'unconscious competence' (*Fig 13.4*).

Fig 13.4 Unconscious Competence

You keep working on your newly acquired skill on a regular basis and find that you get better at doing it. With passage of time, you discover that the skill is now effortless for you and you can actually do it without deliberating on it.

Stuck At Not Being Able

What happens with most people is that they get caught up in the second stage, that is of conscious incompetence and instead of progressing into the third stage, they keep oscillating between the first and second stage of learning. Not to say that people don't read well at all, but even when they know they could read better and use better reading skills for their own progress, they refrain from making an effort in that direction.

Newton's First Law

Making a change in their habits or replacing an old habit with a new one takes quite a lot of doing. Life goes on despite the old habits, causing no threat to survival. Newton's law of inertia then sets in. *Anybody in a state of motion resists any change in its present state of motion until and unless a large enough force is applied to cause a change.*

Readers, therefore are unlikely to just give up on their reading ways, and non-readers, for many known and unknown reasons are unlikely to take to reading without the application of a major drastic force.

Implement What You Know

If you continue implementing your knowledge and understanding of what you have gained through the last few chapters in your reading, whenever you need to read, that in itself will be enough practice to sustain your better reading skills. If you increase your reading per day, there is no reason why you will be one of those who lose out on better reading skills. What has been mentioned in this book is a drop of the ocean. If you decide by yourself to explore other ways of enhancing your reading skills, there is no limit to what you can gain in terms of knowledge, and where you can take yourself in life from where you are today.

Practice Converts Ordinary To Extra Ordinary

Practice is what converts an otherwise ordinary learner into an authoritative genius. Nadia Commancei, the originator of the perfect ten in gymnastics, Sachin Tendulkar, the master blaster and the highest run amasser in cricket, Michael Schumacher, the legendary Formula One race driver, are all examples of diligent regular practice. None of these fore-mentioned champions were born champions though. They all had a purpose, a dream, self-belief, and a passion to excel in whatever they did in life. The singular most common feature of all these champions was regular practice which kept them Match-fit even on an off day.

A Self-champion Is Better Than A Non-champion

You may or may not aspire to have your names alongside such champions. But if you just decide to use their secret to your advantage, you have very little to lose and everything to only gain. Lack of practice can make even champions rusty and if we're in the process of acquiring a new skill, it is in our best interest to consolidate our skill with regular practice.

I'm not recommending long hours of reading or large volumes of reading at a stretch. It certainly helps to do more than just a little reading and to keep implementing the newly acquired learning, techniques and strategies every time you set out to read.

Happy practising. Happy reading!

14 DIFFERENT READING MATERIAL

Different eatables and drinks have to be consumed differently. You would sip a hot coffee, one sip at a time while you would probably drink a cooler soft drink much quicker. Similarly, you would eat a chocolate bar stuffed with nuts even more slowly, chewing and relishing every bite (also wishing in your mind that this would last forever), and you would be happy to quickly gulp down something spicy or bitter.

Different Horses For Different Courses

When you are reading, though it makes good sense to get through the material fast, there may be sections where you may go slower if the terminology or vocabulary is new to you. There may also be sections that you are very familiar with and you would want to get through them more swiftly to save yourself time and energy and protect yourself from boredom.

Reading will be best with a flexibility in your speed and a variability depending on the matter you are tackling. You would perhaps read a poetry or an absorbing piece of literature very slowly, but the journal of your regular work much quicker owing to your familiarity with the content. In the same material, you may accelerate or slow down depending on how comfortable you feel with your comprehension of the matter (*Fig 14.1*).

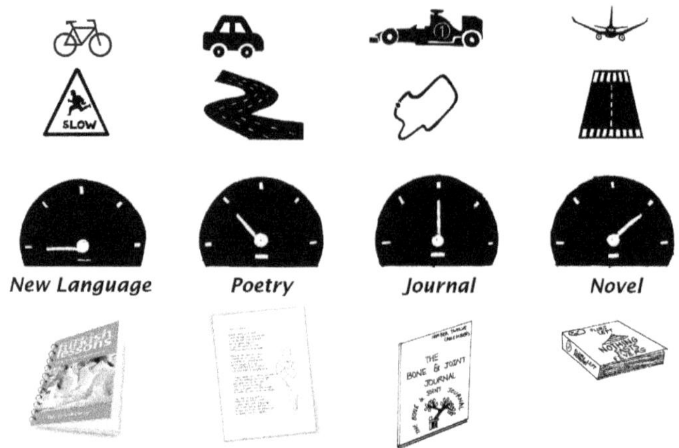

Reading Speed should be flexible depending on familiarity of content

Fig 14.1 Reading Speed Flexibility

The Changing Reading Scenario

The conventional die-hard reader would always prefer the feel of paper between his fingertips, but the reading scenario is changing in a big way. While we mostly read from books, a lot of reading in today's era occurs on screens, desktop monitors, laptops, e-readers, tablets and cell phones, to name a few.

Though most people are apprehensive that reading is dying out, actually with so many gadgets around, people end up having to read a lot more than they ever did. So many youngsters today are constantly communicating through chat applications on their devices that one would not be wrong in saying that more words are being read by this group today, than say twenty-five years ago.

A Reader: A Spotlight For Any Occasion

Be it a social get-together or a more formal work gathering like a conference or a seminar, when people meet during a break, a select few can be the ones holding the attention of a majority. Most others stand around like spectators in awe of the wisdom-filled orator. Amongst the biggest strengths of these popular people is that they are readers (*Fig 14.2*).

Fig 14.2 A Reader is in the spotlight on social occasions.

Flexibility: A Social Advantage

Some of these people realise this and use it to their advantage by indulging in reading, which is not confined to their own field, but stretches to a spectrum of other subjects. Not only does it add to their vocabulary and their street smartness, it also adds in a big way to their 'social and intellectual appeal'. These are the people who are often talked about positively even in their absence. Reading thus, adds more value to the person, not just professionally, but also socially.

15 THE READING ENVIRONMENT

Creating The Reading Environment: The Procedure

Before you start to read, particularly when you have extensive stuff to be read, here are a few things that you need to keep in mind.

Availability of materials. Your study environment should have all the materials you need conveniently placed and easily accessible. It is best to first arrange for all the necessary stationery like your notebook, writing tools (pen, pencil, sketch pens, markers etc.), eraser, a longitude, a launcher, your glasses (if you use one), a bottle of drinking water, a glass, etc. (*Fig 15.1*) so that once you sit down to read, you don't have any interruptions. This increases your enjoyment and allows the brain to 'settle in' comfortably.

Fig 15.1 Availability of Materials

Being prepared as you sit to read will eventually help you improve your concentration and comprehension. Once you get into the flow of reading, having to break the flow for these objects can sometimes be pretty annoying.

Light source. Adequate light is required for reading properly. The best light source is a natural one, preferably sunlight. If one does have to read indoors, it helps to have a light source coming in from behind the reader and not from in front.

Intensity of light should be good enough to illuminate the page, but not too bright to cause a glare that may hurt the reader's eyes. So be careful not to use too bright a bulb if you are using a conventional table lamp as this may hurt the eyes and cause pain and burning of the eyes and even a headache. Sometimes, this too takes the reader away from reading.

Eye-print distance. For most effective reading that does not strain the eyes and that permits reading for longer duration, it is best to keep the printed material at a distance of approximately fifty centimetres from the eyes (*Fig 15.2*). At this distance, it is easier for eyes to focus on groups of words, facilitating acceleration in reading speed. Keeping it closer than fifty centimetres can cause inconvenience to the accommodation system of the eyes and thus, tires the eyes while reading. This limits the amount of reading done in a session.

Fig 15.2 Ideal Eye Print Distance

The only exception to this minimum distance of fifty centimetres is when the print size (font size of the print) is smaller than size-ten font.

Posture. Keeping an 'upright back' has some benefits as it is easier to breathe this way. Comfortable breathing ensures good amount of oxygen taken in by the lungs. That implies a good amount of oxygen reaches the brain. When your body is alert, your brain is alert (*Fig 15.3*).

Fig 15.3 Ideal Reading Posture

Chair and Table. The chair and table that you use for reading should be supporting you and encouraging good posture. The cushions (if any) on the chair should be neither too hard, nor too soft. The back of the chair should ideally be erect and straight. A sloping back causes bad posture and back strain and it also makes proper note-taking uncomfortable.

The seat of the chair should be high enough for thighs to be parallel with floor. This ensures that the main pressure for seating is borne by the main sitting bones at the base of the hips. Both the feet should be resting on the floor. Sitting on very tall chairs with feet dangling in the air tends to make sitting for long periods difficult and causes sensations of tingling and numbness in the lower limbs, which get relieved when the person stands or walks for a while. This again is a distraction and disturbs the smooth flow of reading.

The book should be held in hand at an angle, making it parallel to the face and preventing bending or slouching of the neck towards the table.

With the correct posture, the eyes can make full use of both your central and peripheral vision. This will make reading a fulfilling experience.

Technological gadgets. It helps to have no distractions from your television, music player, cell phone, tablet, or personal computer/laptop around you once you sit down to read (*Fig 15.4*). You should schedule your reading time in such a way that the other things can be kept waiting or for another time and do not interfere with your reading.

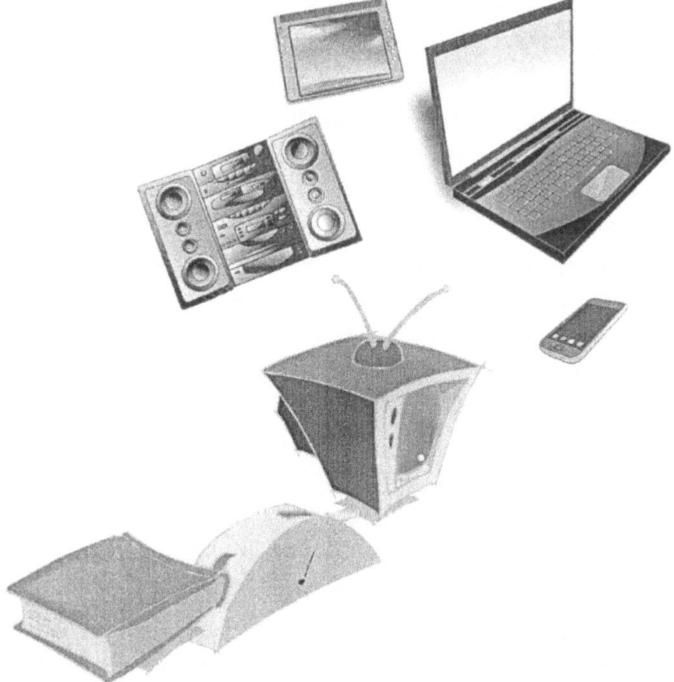

Fig 15.4 Distractions through Gadgets

Some people feel that they perform better when they watch television or have music playing either in the background or in their earphones as they read. This is more a need to continuously be entertained than to facilitate any genuine efficient reading, as we know that whenever there is additional audio input, the brain has to divide its resources between reading and listening. This definitely slows down the reading speed enhancing distraction.

16 ENJOYING THE BENEFITS – GROWING AHEAD FAST

Authority In Your Subject

Fig 16.1 Reading on 1 subject 30 minutes daily for 2 years

Fig 16.2 Reading on 1 subject 60 minutes daily for 1 year

If a person regularly reads on a subject of interest for either thirty minutes every day for two years (*Fig 16.1*) or an hour every day for one year (*Fig 16.2*), that person can become an authority on that subject. Reading is crucial in empowering the person and redirecting him towards success (*Fig 16.3*).

Fig 16.3 Authority on a subject

Technological Innovations

We live in times where innovations in technology are at the forefront of all progress. A reader can keep himself updated with changes and new arrivals on the technological front. Additionally, a reader is more comfortable thumbing through manuals and getting acquainted with new features as well as troubleshooting when something goes wrong (*Fig 16.4*) compared to a non-reader whose reluctance to read can be detrimental to moving ahead. Reading helps in adapting to this constantly changing world.

Fig 16.4 Updated with Technological Innovations

Acquiring New Skills

When educational qualifications of job applicants are at par, it is the other skills that get noticed. It is easier for readers to acquire new skills, be it soft skills, job related skills, or technological know-how (*Fig 16.5*). These skills can also be acquired through coaching institutes or through professional trainers. Therefore, compared to non-readers, readers always have added advantages.

Fig 16.5 Skill acquisition easier for readers

A reader chooses what he wants to improve upon, and is not at the mercy of what the institute offers to teach. Thus, a reader isn't dependent on a coaching class for skill acquisition. Most importantly, the time factor comes in wherein a reader can be flexible and chooses when he needs to work on his skills, unlike a coaching institute which binds a person with their rigid time schedules which are often exceedingly difficult for the already busy learner of today.

Those who are not in the habit of reading regularly may put themselves at risk of becoming the unemployable of the future.

Fig 16.6 Information Explosion

Information Explosion

We live in times of 'information explosion' (*Fig 16.6*). The existing knowledge in any field, thanks to the ongoing hectic research is doubling at an alarming rate every ten years or maybe even earlier. At times, it is not just overwhelming, but often intimidating. A non-reader may keep reacting to changes within the work environment and available resources. On the other hand, the reader has a definite edge, by means of being well-informed and therefore better prepared, and consequently proactive rather than being simply reactive (*Fig 16.7*). The reader acknowledges and deals with the information explosion rather than just being alarmed by it. A reader therefore, excels and decides for his own while a non-reader simply follows what the others do.

Fig 16.7 Being proactive (water) rather than reactive (soda)

Communicating With Others

Your communication skills with people determine the quality of your business life, your family life, and your social life. The working environment today involves working as members of a team as well as having to interact with a varied amount of clients, if one has to make a mark. This involves working effectively with other people of diverse personalities and differing cultural backgrounds. The inability to handle other people effectively and skilfully is a sure-fire recipe for a failing business.

One cannot exist as an island in isolation. One should never see oneself as work completed, instead they should always perceive themselves as work in progress. This will help them be better learners, readers and workers.

It is therefore, imperative that one learns to manage diverse personalities and interpersonal issues as they are bound to emerge. There is good literature available readily for the willing learner to enhance his people-skills, if only one desires to make the effort to read.

A reader will always be at an advantage in acquiring a better understanding of human nature as well as acquiring enhanced people-skills compared to a non-reader who believes that he doesn't need to upgrade himself. While a non-reader would believe in just being there, a reader would want to make a mark for himself.

17 SHARING THE SKILL – MAINTAINING THE HABIT

It is good to be progressive and improve the way we work and live. Humans are often looking for more effective means to achieve the end results. They turn to competent authorities, a book written by an expert or a training workshop where they can learn additional skills. In order to be progressive, they will willingly go through the laborious task of reading a book or attending a workshop, but when it comes to doing something they are not accustomed to, their old thinking pulls them backwards.

General Perceptions

A very common conclusion drawn by many people after they finish reading a self-help book or complete a workshop is:

'All this sounds good to discuss, but is difficult to implement in everyday life.'

'Instead of trying to do this in a new way, which may or may not work for me, it is better to stick to the old tried and tested ways.'

'It is too late now to try and change anything.'

'Had I learned these things earlier, I would have achieved so much more. What is the point now?'

'Why make myself uncomfortable with a new way, when I have been comfortably doing it my way for so long?'

I agree with them on the part, 'difficult to do', because their mind-set is still stuck on their old ways of doing things. Trying to do anything new is going to be a bit challenging, but it's worth trying.

Move Beyond Thinking, Do

But the essence of wanting to improve is having to do something about it and not get restrained by your thinking. On learning a new concept, it is vital that we practice and follow it for a while to reduce the discomfort, and convert it into a pleasurable activity. This can only happen by doing and doing persistently till the desired results are finally achieved.

For doing any task persistently, it is important that we remember the new methods and retain the acquired know-how for a long enough period so that it becomes a part of our system.

Les Giblin, in his very popular book, *Skill with People* mentions three human insights; one of which I am tempted to reproduce here with due acknowledgement and gratitude to the author.

Human Insight #2
How We Retain Information:
10 % of What we Read
20 % of What we Hear
30 % of What we See
50 % of What we See and Hear
70 % of What we Say as we Talk
90 % of What we Say as we Do a thing

In the Human Insight #2, Les Giblin lays stress on how much more information (that is, 90 %) can be retained when we say as we do a thing, compared to just 10 % of what we read. So, if you start implementing what you have read thus far, chances are extremely high that you will retain a significantly larger amount of information that you can put to use even for later. You will then be able to give it enough time, and gradually it will become a habit and routine. It will attain permanence too.

Neuro-psychological Science Confirms

There is a lot of hard core science involved behind this 'insight'.

The nerves that go from the eyes to the brain, called the 'optic nerve' is eighteen times thicker than the 'cochlear nerve' which carries the hearing input from the ears to the brain. So clearly, what we see has distinct advantages over what we hear. But when we do something, even the 'motor cortex' and a whole lot of association areas all over the 'cerebrum' (big brain) as well as the 'cerebellum' (small brain) get involved. When the entire brain is kept busy in the task, there is a higher chance that whatever you are doing is better remembered and therefore better recalled.

Beyond Knowing Now To Retaining For Long

I would stretch this concept a bit and say that the new learning you acquire through constant practice can be consolidated further and thereby, give you additional confidence, if you teach it to someone else. It also impresses other people about how you know such advanced techniques with so much more in-depth understanding. Teaching another person lights up your entire brain and this further consolidates your memory. It helps you retain the concept and also look at the skill in a different light. The best test of whether or not you really understand a concept is trying to teach it to someone else.

Teaching Removes The Possibility Of Self-deceit

More accurately, teaching someone helps you overcome the gaps in your own learning. Your would-be students are the channels through which those gaps will be removed. They will ask questions, along with all sorts of 'what-ifs', and you won't be able to handle them without proper mastery of what you are teaching. When the other person raises doubts and questions, in finding the answers, very often you end up getting acquainted with the subtle intricacies of the skills that were overlooked by you earlier.

When you are forced to grapple with these challenging questions, figuring the answers out for yourself can actually make you see what was earlier unseen by your eyes. Then you can try to explain the answers to others to make sure that this knowledge is etched in your mind. This makes teaching a very powerful tool for cementing your understanding of a subject.

Make A Humble Start

You could start by teaching your siblings, parents, children, friends or colleagues, one concept at a time (*Fig 17.1*). When your new students express their wows and thanks, it adds more value to your own understanding of the concepts and helps you further enhance your skills.

Fig 17.1 Reading Speed Flexibility

What makes you feel good, you tend to do more of.

So, here's wishing a Happy Reading Enhancement to You!

18 FURTHER READING ENHANCEMENT

Here are a few books that I had read on my journey of becoming a speed reader (*Fig 18.1*). They have motivated me to take this generously humanitarian skill across to more reading enthusiasts.

Fig 18.1 Becoming A Speed Reader

Princeton Language Institute and Abby Marks Beale **10 Days to Faster Reading**: Warner Books

Tina Konstant **Speed Reading in a Week**: Chartered Management Institute, Hodder and Stoughton

Nicholas Reid Schaffzin The Princeton Review **Reading Smart** Advanced Techniques for Improved Reading: Random House Inc.

Kathryn Redway **How To Be a Rapid Reader**: Viva Books Private Limited

Rick Ostrov **Power Reading**: Education Press

Roz Townsend **Read with Speed** Six Easy Steps: Emerald Publishers

Wade E Cutler **Triple Your Reading Speed** The Accele Read Method: Thomson Arco

Abby Marks Beale with *Pam Mullan* **The complete Idiot's Guide to Speed Reading**: Alpha

H. Bernard Wechsler and *Arthur H. Bell* **Speed Reading for Professionals**: Barron's A Business Success Guide

Burke Hedges **Read & Grow** Rich How the hidden power of reading can make you richer in all areas of your life!: INTI Publishing & Resource Books, Inc.

Gordon Wainwright **Read Faster Recall More** Use Proven Techniques for Speed Reading and Maximum Recall: How to Books Ltd.

Geoffrey A Dudley **Speed Reading** Jaico Publishing House

Howard Stephen Berg and *Marcus Conyers* **Speed-reading The Easy Way** Barron's

Norman Lewis **How to Get more Out of Your Reading**: Goyal Saab

Tony Buzan **The Speed Reading Book** BBC

ABOUT THE AUTHOR

Dr. Hozefa A Bhinderwala is a practicing Consultant Psychiatrist for the last 20 years providing his services presently to Prince Aly Khan Hospital, Saifee Hospital and Global Hospitals in Mumbai. He has also served as an Expert Medical Adviser for the Neuropsychiatry division of Marksans Pharma for more than 3 years. He has been a School Counsellor for Multiple Schools of different boards for over a decade.

After the launch of his first book *Speed Read* in 2006, he has helped thousands of students and participants through his Reading Enhancement Workshops, which he continues even now. He is passionate about public speaking, making his own videos, presentations, and motivating young minds. His active involvement in religious programmes across communities stems from his ability to simplify neuroscience into easy to chew nuggets facilitating learning. He is a voracious reader and infuses enthusiasm and motivation in those with whom he interacts. Besides writing, he has been actively involved in creating awareness to fight the prevalent stigma about mental health illnesses and reluctance of people to seek help for psychological difficulties. He is a big fan of the power of story-telling and the immense potential of You Tube videos in helping him achieve his destigmatizing efforts.

He resides in South Mumbai with his wife Tasneem, daughter Fatema and son Taher

www.ingramcontent.com/pod-product-compliance
Ingram Content Group UK Ltd.
Pitfield, Milton Keynes, MK11 3LW, UK
UKHW021331070726
13610UKWH00011B/28

9 789386 141361